Beyond
BUSINESS
CASUAL

◆

WHAT TO
WEAR TO WORK
IF YOU WANT
TO GET AHEAD

◆

ANN MARIE SABATH

ASJA Press
New York   Lincoln   Shanghai

TEXAS STATE TECH. COLLEGE
LIBRARY-SWEETWATER TX.

Beyond Business Casual
What To Wear To Work If You Want To Get Ahead

All Rights Reserved © 2000, 2004 by Ann Marie Sabath

No part of this book may be reproduced or transmitted in any form or by any means, graphic, electronic, or mechanical, including photocopying, recording, taping, or by any information storage retrieval system, without the written permission of the publisher.

ASJA Press
an imprint of iUniverse, Inc.

For information address:
iUniverse, Inc.
2021 Pine Lake Road, Suite 100
Lincoln, NE 68512
www.iuniverse.com

Originally published by Career Press

Cover design by Cheryl Finbow

ISBN: 0-595-30653-5

Printed in the United States of America

ACKNOWLEDGMENTS

To my son Scott, who lent a Generation X perspective to this book.

My dear friend, Lillian Hawkins, who helped me through the final hours of writing this book.

John J. O'Sullivan, an editor at Career Press, who designed the book saw it through to the end.

And to my faithful writing companion, Micah—our four-year old miniature schnauzer, who remained at my side even in the wee hours of the morning as I was writing this book.

CONTENTS

Chapter 5:

❚INTRODUCTION

Welcome to *Beyond Business Casual: What To Wear To Work If You Want To Get Ahead.* This book is about how your clothes speak for you. Knowing what to wear and when to wear is a learned skill. Some people learn it by emulation; others by default. Others don't have a clue about what to wear and when.

In the 1970s, dressing in business was as simple as putting together an outfit by mixing and matching clothes. Today, with business casual on the scene, "dress-down" days have become a liability for many individuals and organizations alike. Although some companies may not have a clear-cut set of rules regarding what is considered appropriate, those that do may not enforce the guidelines for fear of damaging an employee's ego and perhaps even provoking a sexual harassment or discrimination suit.

Beyond Business Casual will help you look the part of an executive and achieve your professional goals by:

◆ Showing how to make a terrific first impression.
◆ Demonstrating through your appearance that you pay attention to detail.
◆ Helping you to make good judgments on what is considered appropriate.
◆ Teaching you to err on the side of conservatism when you're unsure of how to dress for an unprecedented occasion.

◆ Assisting you in recognizing what the "dress culture" is in the organization you're representing.

◆ Showing you key ways for climbing that slippery ladder of success by the way you look.

This book was written by someone who didn't own a business suit until she was 30 years old. Teaching high school was a great career, but disciplining kids both at school and at home was not what I considered fun. However, I knew if I was to make the transition into the business scene, a visual change was in order. By watching how the "old boys' network" dressed and learning the secrets of those women who seemed to get and keep their foot in the right doors, I built a wardrobe that spoke the language of the organizations I was visiting.

After 15 years of watching, doing, and teaching others the secrets to making their wardrobes work for them, I realize that it is as easy as reciting the alphabet.

Today, what some people wear to work is questionable. Their taste—or lack thereof—raises many an eyebrow. In fact in some organizations, it's difficult to tell the CEO from the custodian, based on the way the fearless leader comes dressed for work.

Dress rules have certainly changed dramatically during the past few decades. In fact, there have been so many transitions regarding what is considered both acceptable and appropriate that many people are confused about what to wear to work. Could it be that their companies do not have a written set of guidelines? Or could it be that the dress code in print is just not followed? And when employees create their own set of dress rules, how does upper management handle it?

Beyond Business Casual is the ideal guide for anyone who wants success through dress. It is a must for you if :

◆ You have been wearing suits your entire life and your organization has converted to business casual attire one or more days a week.

◆ You are very competent, yet your mode of dress doesn't reflect your abilities.

◆ You are graduating from college and want to learn how to transition from the jean scene to the workplace.

◆ You are re-entering the workforce.

◆ You are a spouse and/or "significant other" and wonder what you should wear to business functions.

◆ You travel for business and wonder what you should wear en route.

Most people "don't know what they don't know" and sabotage their careers by the way they dress for work. For that reason, this book puts those unwritten rules in black and white once and for all. It is meant to help budding professionals and seasoned employees alike in climbing the ladder of success rather than tripping on a wrung based on how they look.

This book has been designed to "button down" those unwritten rules. It has been written to guide companies' decision-makers in setting appropriate dress standards for their organizations. It helps employees recognize if what they are wearing to work is inappropriate and shows them what is considered "business appropriate" for their organizations. Finally, this book teaches that "business professional" attire has not gone by the wayside and explains the times a suit should be worn.

Beyond Business Casual also has been written to let employees know that business casual dress and ironing *do* go hand in hand. Business casual dress does not equate with the same comfortable clothes you throw on when you get home from work.

Beyond Business Casual presents a series of chapters with several topics addressed in each section. You can go through the book sequentially or skim through the contents or index and find the section that speaks to you.

As you read through the material, you will see real-life questions asked from our "Success in Dress" workshop participants. Many of the questions have also been asked by individuals who have been sent to professional coaching classes to learn how to look the part of the organization they represent. You will read questions from individuals who have made it...and from those who don't understand that they weren't hired based on their appearance. My goal for sharing the answers to these commonly-asked questions is to spare you an embarrassing moment and perhaps even assist you in securing that job or business opportunity by looking the part!

HOW DID THIS
DRESSING DILEMMA EVER BEGIN?

It appears that this dressing dilemma was created when companies instituted "dress-down" days. Mistake number one was that many human resource directors and company decision-makers assumed employees knew what was considered "business appropriate." Because many companies chose not to establish dress code policies, they soon watched people show up for work in what they wear to the grocery store, soccer game, etc. They also witnessed employees march into work wearing clothes that weren't ironed (even permanent press needs to be touched up) and in fabrics that are more suitable for "casual" rather than "business casual" environments (such as leather, denim, etc.).

POLICIES ARE ONLY AS GOOD
AS WHAT IS ENFORCED

Supervisors in companies with written dress-code policies aren't always sure how to enforce them. They ask, "Should a person be sent home for not dressing appropriately?" "How can I tell a lower-level person not to wear certain clothes when our senior managers dress worse?" "As a male manager, how can I tell a woman that her skirt is way too short without being accused of sexual harassment?"

Where is business dress headed in this new millennium? Will business casual remain the norm rather than the exception? Or will business professional once again be the order of the day? Many people wonder, "Where have all the dress rules gone?" Many organizations with the best services or products since the invention of sliced bread have employees who come across as looking more "schlocky" than the used-car salesman down the street.

Although we may be in a new millennium, it looks like we're back to the basics when it comes to teaching people what is considered appropriate dress. That includes defining the differences among business professional, business casual, and casual attire. It also means knowing whose dress to emulate if you want to climb your organization's ladder of success...and whose dress to mimic if you want to sabotage your career.

The goal of this book is to assist people in going *beyond* business casual. It's for those individuals who want to get ahead and are interested in knowing what clothes will help them to do just that. This book is divided into the following chapters:

1. **Let's Start at the Very Beginning: What Does "Dressing" Mean?**
2. **How Your Dress Affects Your Productivity**
3. **What Kind of Dress Attitude Are You Projecting?**
4. **Tips for Men on the Climb**
5. **Tips for Women Climbing the Ladder of Success**
6. **Much Ado About Nothing?**
7. **Dressing for Job Interviews**
8. **Commanding Presence on Business Casual Days**
9. **What to Wear During Videoconferences**
10. **How to Command that "21st Century" Presence**
11. **Travel and Dress: Key Ways for Dressing on the Run**

12. **The Art of Dressing Appropriately When Doing Business Abroad**

What makes *Beyond Business Casual* different from what's on the market?

1. This book is written in a question-and-answer format so that readers can glance at tips based on the topic of their choice.

2. It provides an updated look on how attire affects their performance, productivity and ultimately a company's profits.

3. Questions are asked by CEOs, personnel directors, and new hires who want to know what is considered appropriate dress.

4. This book offers readers access to our toll-free business dress hotline and compatible business dress e-mail line which will allow them to have their dress-related questions answered about what is considered appropriate attire.

Beyond Business Casual has been written to help you get ahead. It's been created to put a focus on what to wear to work if you want to climb the corporate ladder of success.

While many people do what they love and love what they do, others wouldn't take going to work that far. Still others put in a good day's work and clock out promptly at ending time. Finally, others have just graduated from college or finished raising a family and are back at square one when it comes to knowing what to wear. No matter which of these situations describes you, this book will definitely help you to create an image based on where you want to be in your career.

After you read this book, if you still have a question that you would like to have answered, please remember that I am only a telephone call or a few keystrokes away. Call me at 800-873-9909 or e-mail your question to me at:

beyondbusinesscasual @ateaseinc.com

Happy Reading!

–Ann Marie Sabath
March 2000

CHAPTER 1

LET'S START AT THE VERY BEGINNING: WHAT DOES "DRESSING" MEAN?

 THE 10 MOST COMMONLY MADE DRESS RULE INFRACTIONS:

1. Not recognizing that the clothing you buy should be purchased for long-term wear.
2. Confusing casual clothes with "grunge."
3. Wearing clothes that are less than clean and crisp on business casual day.
4. Wearing clothes that do not match.
5. Choosing a garment that is not flattering to your body shape.
6. Keeping clothes that you have not worn for more than two years.
7. Not recognizing that you are judged by the way you dress.
8. Not realizing that every organization has a dress culture—even if it is an unwritten one.
9. Not choosing a dress mentor within your organization.
10. Considering tennis shoes to be business-casual attire when they are casual.

HUH? DRESSING?

Question: Please give me the definition of "dressing."

Answer: In the strictest sense of the word, "dressing" is the process of covering your body with garments that will shield it from damaging forces. It involves choosing clothes that are conducive to the environment where these items will be worn. Your choices should be based on your industry and what your role models wear. Your own definition of dressing should be based on the way you want to be perceived by others and your interest in growing within your organization.

Dressing is such a basic skill for every individual that it's essential you see how critical it is to your well-being. Your new sensitivity will assist you in looking and feeling your best as you put on your work gear each day.

CLOTHES AS INVESTMENTS

Question: Which clothes are the best investments?

Answer: It's been said that the clothes that are the best buy are the ones that you wear the most. How many times have you bought clothes and accompanying items (such as shoes, jewelry, etc.) that have been worn less than you can count on one hand? If you went into your closet right now, how many items could you say you have worn at least once during the last year? If you haven't worn items at least once during the last year, take them out of your closet and give them to charity or sell them to a consignment shop.

Brenda Layton, an acquaintance of mine who does a great job putting her business wardrobe together has developed the "Four Cs" when deciding which clothes to buy for work. Keep these tips in mind when developing your image in your wardrobe:

1. **Correct and appropriate:** Be sure your attire is correct and appropriate for your work setting. *Casual* does not equate with *grunge*. If you are usually required to wear a business suit, jeans are probably not appropriate. Perhaps khakis and a shirt or sweater would be more appropriate.

2. **Crisp and clean:** Be sure everything is well pressed, neat, and clean. Shoes should be polished.

3. **Coordination:** Only purchase garments that will correspond with two other items you already own. By doing so, everything else matches, allowing you to expand your wardrobe.

4. **Complementary:** Make sure everything fits and complements your figure. Pants or tops that are too tight for women are definite "no-no's" When necessary, purchase clothes a size larger.

DO YOU HAVE CLUTTER IN YOUR CLOSET?

Question: I have such a hard time parting with clothes I haven't worn. Is there a logical way to get rid of them?

Answer: You bet. Some rainy day—in the near future—dig into your closet. Divide clothes, shoes and accessories into two sections: Those which you have worn even once during the past two years and those you haven't worn for the last two years. Either pack all of the items that fall into the second category for your local consignment store or give them to charity.

Now look at the remaining clothes that are left in your closet and drawers. You still probably have more items than you know what to do with. Take stock of what you have by categorizing them into what you wear to work when you are dressing professionally, what you wear during dress-down days, what you wear for leisure, what you wear when you are running errands, and finally what you wear when you are home wearing your "Velveteen Rabbit" clothes (those outfits that you would only want your family and friends to see you in).

Now that you have completed this exercise, you may see the items that you have chosen to keep a bit differently. Instead of keeping clothes to which you are attached emotionally, you now see them from a functional standpoint. You have given them a purpose for hanging there or for taking up valuable closet space.

DRESSING IS A MENTAL THING

 Question: Why do people judge you by the way you dress? It seems to me that dressing is only a skin-deep way of looking at a person.

A **Answer:** Besides being important to dress according to your organization's "culture," what you wear is also a reflection of your self-esteem and association with others. It also plays a vital role in the first impression that you give others.

Here's a test to prove my point: Go to your nearest mall and people-watch for a few minutes. Select three people who appear to be waiting for someone. Now, if you needed to borrow money from one of them, which person would you approach? Why? If you needed directions, which person would you approach? Why? If you needed a shoulder to cry on, which person would you approach? Why?

"STYLE IS THE DRESS OF THOUGHTS."

—PHILIP DORMER STANHOPE, EARL OF CHESTERFIELD

Now of the three people, who would stop to listen to your request and answer it? Why? What impression of believability are your choice in clothes projecting for you?

What Dressing Appropriately Can Do For You

Question: Why is there such an important emphasis on "dressing the part"?

Answer:

In business, actions have always spoken louder than words—this will never change. A mastery of dressing appropriately can mean the difference between getting a job, climbing the ladder in your organization, getting an appointment, or securing a contract. Why settle for less when it takes the same amount of energy to do what will make things much easier for you?

> *"As we slip into our costumes each morning we slip into our roles."*
>
> —Anonymous

WHAT HAPPENS
WHEN YOU DON'T DRESS THE PART?

Q Question: Is it possible to dress down and still be taken seriously? Business professional clothes have been my suit of armor for so long that I'm not sure how to act when dressed in business casual clothes.

A Answer: Even when you are dressed down, you can still do so in a way that maintains your professional demeanor, rather than dressing in a haphazard manner. One way to dress down while still feeling dressed up is to invest in the same high quality of business casual apparel that you do when investing in business professional clothes.

TUNING INTO
AN ORGANIZATION'S DRESS CULTURE

Q Question: What is the best way to tune into the dress culture of an organization?

A Answer: Typically, an organization's dress culture is dictated from the tone set by upper management or by people hosting an event. When a dress culture is not written in an organization's procedure manual or noted on an invitation, err on the side of conservative in your choice of dress rather than committing a dressing gaffe.

If you've been to a company or know someone who is upper-level management in that organization, what did you notice to be the dress culture of the office? What did you wear? Did you feel that it was a good choice or would you have worn something else if you had realized what people there were going to be wearing?

LETTING YOUR ETHNICITY SHOW

Question: How can I maintain my ethnicity when dressing for work?

Answer: The main rule is to look professional at all times. If your choice of ethnic hairstyle and dress meets your organization's guidelines, you'll be fine. Keep in mind that your overall look should reflect the same attention to detail you projected when interviewing for the position you have today.

WHO TO ASK ABOUT DRESS POLICIES

Question: When first beginning at a new organization, who should I ask about what is considered appropriate?

Answer: Try asking the human resource director or the person who offered you the job. These individuals will be able to guide you in the right direction regarding their organization's dress expectations.

ATTIRE FOR PRESENTATIONS

Q Question: When giving a presentation, I'm always unsure of how I should dress. A few weeks ago, I was the presenter for a program. As a few other individuals and I were setting out handouts prior to the session, the hotel's audio-visual person walked into the room to do a microphone check. Rather than approaching me, this person assumed a person wearing a blazer was the presenter. I found it to be a very humbling experience and need your advice. Do you have any suggestions?

A **Answer:** There's not a better teacher than living proof. In the situation you described, you witnessed that the individual commanding the most "presence" was perceived to be the presenter.

In order to make sure you are commanding presence, always dress "one notch up." By doing so, your program participants—and audio-visual people alike—will know that you are the presenter the moment they see you.

TODAY'S MOST COMMON DRESS FAUX PAS

Question: What are the most commonly made dress faux pas that you see?

Answer: You asked for them and here they are:

1. Not realizing that your work competency is measured by how you dress.
2. Wearing casual clothes on business casual days.
3. Wearing poorly maintained clothes on business casual day.
4. Believing that permanent-press clothes do not need to be ironed.
5. Not recognizing that the way to show up dressed for work is based on what your manager wears, rather than what your colleagues are wearing.
6. Wearing rubber-soled shoes rather than soles made of leather.
7. Considering a "scrunchie" to be an appropriate hair accessory for work.
8. Not having a business professional outfit with you—even on those business casual days.
9. Not recognizing that the way you maintain your shoes is equated with how well you pay attention to detail with your work projects.

CHAPTER 2

HOW YOUR DRESS AFFECTS YOUR PRODUCTIVITY

 THE 10 MOST COMMONLY MADE MISTAKES WHEN GETTING IT TOGETHER:

1. Not maintaining tinted hair as often as necessary.
2. Not having an emergency business professional outfit at the office for unexpected client meetings.
3. Not recognizing that your accessories add "presence" to your outfit.
4. Not realizing that the impression people have of you by what you wear can make or break your professional reputation.
5. Not realizing that the clothes you buy should work for you rather than you working for them (such as linen).
6. Not remembering that your hands are the second thing people notice about you. (Your face is the first.)
7. Not investing in a trench coat with a zip-out lining, allowing it to double as a winter coat.
8. Not keeping an umbrella in your car, at your office, or with your travel gear for an unexpected downpour.
9. Carrying a wallet overflowing with receipts.
10. Not having your palm pilot or daily planner with you at all times.

DRESSING WELL INCREASES PRODUCTIVITY

Question: Do you believe that the way you dress really affects your productivity?

Answer: When I was in high school (a long, long time ago) I had a friend named Marcia. I remember on one particular occasion I wasn't feeling so well. Either I had a cold, the flu, or I was just feeling a little down (I don't remember the reason anymore). However, Marcia said something to me that I will never forget. She told me that whenever she's feeling sick or a little low, she dresses up to make herself feel better. This could mean wearing a nice outfit, her favorite shirt, styling her hair, or all of the above.

The reason I remember her saying this is because it actually worked! It doesn't take a rocket scientist (or even a high school kid) to figure out the way you dress affects the way you feel about yourself. But could the clothes you wear effect your productivity? And if so, to what extent?

William Shakespeare once said, "All the world is a stage and all the men and women merely players." I may not view life through the same paradigm

> "EVERY TIME YOU OPEN YOUR WARDROBE, YOU LOOK AT YOUR CLOTHES AND WONDER WHAT YOU ARE GOING TO WEAR. WHAT YOU ARE REALLY SAYING IS, 'WHO AM I GOING TO BE TODAY?'"
>
> —FAY WELDON, *NEW YORKER* JUNE 26, 1995

as Shakespeare, but I do believe the clothes we wear greatly influence the roles we play in life (and the way in which we play them). One example of this is the rapid increase in business casual dress throughout North America. Many claim that the switch to business casual, whether it's dress-down Fridays or five days a week, has positively influenced company culture and morale. However, in my opinion, the jury is still out.

ADD CLOUT TO WHAT YOU SAY
BY WHAT YOU WEAR

Q Question: What clothes can I wear that will give me more clout in the office?

A Answer: The best advice I can give you is to wear tailored clothes. If your organization encourages business professional dress, suits are the name of the game. However, if your organization is like most, business casual is worn at least one day each week. In this case, continue to wear tailored clothing following the one-notch-down rule.

"NOWADAYS, IF MEN ARE MORE SERIOUS THAN WOMEN, IT'S BECAUSE THEIR CLOTHES ARE DARKER."

—ANDRE GIDE

You also will add clout to what you say by always being impeccable in your dress and hygiene. By that I mean wearing maintained shoes, making sure that you get a haircut before looking like you need one, and making sure that your nails are well manicured at all times.

YOUR CLOTHES AS A CONFIDENCE METER

Question: How can clothes make you feel more confident?

Answer: When you look the part, you tend to feel better about yourself, thus projecting a more confident attitude. In turn, this confidence carries over to the words you use and the way people perceive you. The next time you put on an outfit, ask yourself if it makes you feel the part that you want to project that day (such as presenter, counselor, decision-maker, etc.).

POWER COLORS 101

Question: What colors can help you command presence?

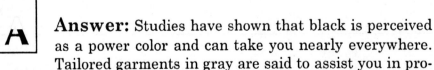

Answer: Studies have shown that black is perceived as a power color and can take you nearly everywhere. Tailored garments in gray are said to assist you in projecting authority. Finally, tailored garments in navy are thought to be a nonintimidating color.

An attorney in a court of law will frequently wear a navy suit when he or she is adressing a jury.

Showing that you mean business

Question: What are some dress tips that say "I mean business"?

Answer: Below are six recommendations that may assist you in projecting that "I mean business" attitude:

1. Invest in the best quality clothing you can afford. Remember, less is really more.
2. Recognize that dark colors can take you just about everywhere and tend to be more versatile than lighter-colored clothing.
3. Command presence through your accessories. Once again, buy the classics investing in quality items or, at minimum, "look-a-likes."
4. Recognize that the way you maintain your nails can add or detract from your overall look.
5. Never underestimate the power of well-maintained shoes. Shoes definitely can make or break an outfit.
6. Always follow the "Rule of 13." In other words, wear enough accessories to command presence, yet no more than 13. Otherwise, your accessories may become distractions rather than accessories. (For more information on the "Rule of 13," turn to page 93.)

WORKING AT HOME

Q Question: I work from home and don't see a need for getting dressed up each morning before going into my back bedroom and sitting down at my desk. Until my company gets us hooked up with video monitors, I see no reason for expending the energy to get dressed up. Suggestions?

A **Answer:** In a recent international study about tele-commuting attire, it was found that individuals working from home tended to dress down. Their attire included jeans, weekend attire, and business casual clothes. A few people who were brutally honest even admitted that their attire ranged from their birthday suit to anything they could get their hands on before the phone started to ring.

My best advice to you is to be sure to wear something that puts you in a professional frame of mind. By wearing clothes that make you feel businesslike, your words and work style will reflect a similar attitude.

THE SECRET TO LOOKING PROMOTABLE

Question: What is the secret to looking promotable?

Answer: Easy, look around. Take note of what recently promoted individuals within your organization are wearing. Are they dressed like the CEO of your organization? If so, follow suit.

WHERE HAVE ALL

THE ROLE MODELS GONE?

Question: What if there are no role models around me to emulate?

Answer: In that case, dress for the position you want rather than for the one you have. By doing so, those around you may associate you with the position in which individuals may have to dress more conservatively.

UPDATED CLASSICS

Question: My taste in clothes is richer than my budget. How can I make my taste and budget compatible?

Answer: Melody Gensler, owner of Melody's (a wonderful women's boutique in Milwaukee) has a perfect answer for blending your taste and wallet. She recommends that you build your wardrobe by investing in "updated classic" clothes—clothes that are in style for many years due to their timeless look.

BEING PREPARED

FOR UNEXPECTED MEETINGS

Question: I've been in situations where I showed up for work only to learn that a last-minute meeting had been scheduled that required business professional attire. How can I prevent this from happening in the future?

Answer: Easy. From now on, be better prepared. Have a change of clothes available either in your workspace or car trunk. This way, when you are asked to fill in for someone and realize that a more formal outfit is in order, you can make the switch. By having another set of clothes accessible, you will never have to apologize for how you look.

CHAPTER 3

WHAT KIND OF DRESS ATTITUDE ARE YOU PROJECTING?

 THE 10 MOST COMMONLY MADE "DRESS ATTITUDE" MISTAKES

1. Not immediately removing a hat when walking into a building.
2. Not knowing that glasses frames are meant to enhance your appearance—as well as allowing you to see.
3. Not owning a pair of leather gloves for the winter.
4. Using an umbrella that is on its last spoke.
5. Wearing a pair of shoes in winter slush when boots are more appropriate.
6. Wearing jewelry that distracts—rather than enhances—the rest of your outfit.
7. Wearing a belt that does not match your shoes.
8. Not maintaining your briefcase (computer case) as well as you maintain your shoes.
9. Not knowing that your nails are noticed second only to your face.
10. Wearing lighter colors, which project a more casual look.

WEARING GLASSES

 Question: Is wearing glasses out and contacts "in"? I prefer glasses yet I am concerned that I am not projecting an updated image.

Answer: It's your choice. If you choose to wear glasses rather than contacts, be sure to select a frame that complements the shape of your face and coloring. The advantage of wearing glasses is to assist you in projecting a more serious look. Also, if you interact with individuals much older than you, eyewear can assist you in being taken more seriously.

Finally, when choosing lenses you will be wearing indoors, be sure to choose clear rather than tinted lenses. People who wear tinted lenses indoors are perceived to have a "shady" appearance. After all, clear lenses allow you maintain better eye contact with others.

> "A GOOD PAIR OF GLASSES WILL ALTER YOUR PERCEPTION OF OTHERS. A BAD PAIR OF GLASSES WILL CHANGE OTHERS' PERCEPTION OF YOU."
>
> —SCOTT WERT, COLUMNIST, "ON THE JOB WITH GENERATION X," CINCINNATI DOWNTOWNER

DO COLORS
REALLY AFFECT YOUR MOOD?

Question: I feel so alive in bright colors and so drab in lighter ones. Is there truth to the notion that colors affect your mood?

Answer: It's certainly not your imagination. Not only will some colors make you feel better or worse based on your mood, certain ones will also assist you in looking better when you wear tones that enhance your skin tone. For instance, individuals with darker skin and hair tones tend to look more vibrant in brighter colors.

An image consultant will be able to assist you in identifying colors that will continue to make you look and feel good.

REGIONALISMS

Question: Do people dress differently in different parts of the United States?

Answer: They certainly do. In the southern part of the country, women tend to dress up more and make a point of accessorizing their clothes. In some parts of the Southwest, you may see boots and string ties, in place of shoes and neckties. On the East coast, individuals tend to dress up. For that reason, business casual day will be much less formal in companies in the Midwest and on the west coast. Midwesterners tend to be very unpretentious about their clothing. While they may wear either business professional or business casual clothes, many tend to take a more down-to-earth and practical approach to dress than in other parts of the nation.

Looking like a clone

Question: When representing a conservative company, is it mandatory to look like a corporate clone by wearing what most people wear to work?

Answer: If you want to do the politically correct thing and intend to grow within a conservative organization, I'd suggest emulating the dress of the people whose positions you aspire to have. Remember, what you know is important; however, it is just as important to package yourself properly.

IMAGE CONSULTANTS

Q Question: I realize that I am far from gifted when it comes to coordinating outfits, styling my hair, and doing my makeup. To my embarrassment, however, my boss has been dropping some hints that relate to my appearance. I spoke with a friend about the situation and she suggested I contact an image consultant. Isn't that a little extreme? I thought that only actors, musicians, and politicians used image consultants.

A **Answer:** Image consultants are used by the average person much more than one would believe. A qualified image consultant will be able to assist you in looking the part that you are trying to achieve.

If you are interested in enhancing your image, consider investing in yourself by meeting with an image consultant. However, before contacting one make a list of where you aspire to be professionally and the "image" you'd like to acquire in order to begin looking the part. When you are ready to contact an image consultant, be sure to screen individuals carefully. Confirm that the person is an Association of Image Consultants International (AICI) member. Also, check references to learn how the image consultant was able to assist others in developing a new look. Finally, once you share your objectives with your image consultant, be sure to get the hourly fee and allotted amount of time in writing. This will help you avoid surprises later.

THE IMPORTANCE
OF TACT AND DIPLOMACY

 Question: One of the individuals on my top management team is rather rough around the edges when it comes to grooming. As a male manager, how can I drop the hint to her without bruising her ego or setting myself up for a sexual harassment suit?

Answer: If you are this person's manager, discuss this area of concern during her next performance appraisal. Give concrete examples where this person can improve.

If you are uncomfortable bringing up this topic with this woman, ask one of your female counterparts to discuss it as part of a "woman-to-woman" conversation. This may help.

DRESSING AND AGE

Q Question: As an ambitious and successful individual, I also happen to be one of the youngest account executives at our investment firm. It just so happens that my very conservative boss is twice my age. Although I meet deadlines and complete projects with flying colors, I don't feel that I get the respect I have earned. I've been in this job one year. My boss still factors in my age when delegating tasks and portfolios to my colleagues and me. He thinks that many of his long-term clients will have as much of a problem with my age as he does, even though he is the only person I know who has this issue. What can I do to appear older?

A Answer: Based on what you are telling me, it sounds like you perceive this issue to be an age factor. However, there's a good chance that your situation may involve your youthful image more than your age.

Although I do not know the dress code at the organization you represent, most financial institutions and investment companies are rather conservative in their dress. For that reason, I'd recommend the following:

1. If you aren't already doing so, mirror what your boss wears. If he wears business professional attire to work, you should too.
2. If your boss removes his jacket when he's in his office yet always seems to be wearing it when he leaves the department, so should you.

3. Even if you wear contacts, buy a pair of nonprescription glasses with nonreflective lenses. Wearing glasses may give you a more serious—and older—look.

4. Finally, make sure you invest in quality clothes, and good shoes that are well-maintained.

HEADPHONES

Q **Question: When traveling to and from work on the train, I wear headphones to block out the noise around me. When I get to work, I find that I can be more productive when listening to music through my headphones. Because I don't share a workspace, I can't see how I'm bothering anyone. What's your opinion on wearing headphones at work?**

A **Answer:** Although it sounds like you are more productive wearing headphones, there are a few questions that should be asked. What about those people who are within an earshot of you? Is the music that you're listening to so loud that it may be distracting others? What about when a person a few feet away has a question for you—can you hear that person?

It seems to me that by wearing headphones, you are closing off your communication with those around you. While it may be an enhancement for you, it may be perceived as a distraction for others. Try talking to your manager and those around you to get their opinions on how they feel when you use headphones.

RINGS ON YOUR FINGERS...
AND IN YOUR NOSE?

Question: As you probably know, today's youth are into body piercing. I am graduating from college this spring with a bachelor's degree in business and a master's degree in accounting. I have a stud in my nose and an eyebrow ring. I enjoy this jewelry just as other women enjoy a meaningful necklace or a ring with sentimental value.

These piercings are more than just jewelry; they are expressions of myself. How does body piercing fit into today's business fashion? Is there a place for such accessories? If so, when and where?

Answer: There is certainly a place for rings on your fingers and in your brows and nose: When your manager shows up for work wearing similar adornments.

Because you are graduating with both a business degree and with a graduate degree in accounting, I'm led to believe that you may be entering a more conservative field, one that doesn't encourage such adornments. If you aren't willing to remove or cover your piercings for work, you might want to consider looking for a position in a field where body piercing is more readily accepted.

WHAT ABOUT FABRICS?

Question: Are there certain fabrics that are considered business professional material?

Answer: Wool gabardine, silk, cotton, and oxford for shirts are fabrics that give a very polished appearance. Most other fabrics tend to give a more casual look. Whether you are dressed in business professional or "dress down" attire, invest in clothes of the highest quality fabric you can possibly afford.

WHAT ABOUT LIGHTER COLORS?

Question: Do lighter colors project a more casual look?

Answer: While you may still be taken seriously with lighter colors, they may project a more casual look. Of course, your overall look will also be based on the type of fabric, the quality of fabric, and how your clothes are tailored.

THE SCRUNCH TEST

Question: I have such a limited amount of time. What tips do you have for selecting high-quality, low-maintenance clothes?

Answer: Good question. The easiest way to make your clothes work for you begins when you purchase them. Before you take a garment from the rack, test it to be sure it passes the "scrunch" test. Squeeze the fabric. When you release it, is it wrinkled? If it is, move on to another item. The scrunch test is the true test for knowing how even the most well-pressed item will look at a 3 p.m. meeting after wearing it for several hours.

A WORD ABOUT GRAYING HAIR

Question: My hair is turning gray and I'm not sure if I want to begin coloring it. Is there a stigma attached to having gray hair?

Answer: Covering your gray hair is a personal preference. While some people are adamant about dying their hair at the first sign of grayness, others are perfectly comfortable allowing their hair to grow in naturally.

The stigma attached to gray hair can vary with your profession and market you're trying to reach. For example, if you are recruiting college students and you want to look youthful, go for the bottle. If you are selling life insurance to senior citizens, your gray may lend a helping hand.

The best advice I can give you is to do what makes you feel the most comfortable. However, if you choose to cover up that gray be sure to maintain it.

THE NAPE OF YOUR NECK

Question: The hair on the nape of my neck seems to need more attention than the hair on the rest of my head. Any suggestions?

Answer: If you live with someone, ask that person to use your electric razor to shave those hairs from the nape of your neck between hair appointments.

ON THE SUBJECT OF DANDRUFF

Question: What can be done about dandruff? I seem to have a slight case of it and try to wear light colors so it is less noticeable on my shirt.

Answer: Rather than keeping those dark colors in the closet, buy a medicated shampoo that will help you to eliminate dandruff. If that doesn't help, seek professional advice from a dermatologist who may be able to prescribe a shampoo for your scalp that may be more effective.

KEEP YOUR COLOGNE
AND PERFUME TO YOURSELF

 Question: My cubicle mate wears what he considers to be a terrific cologne. He puts so much of it on that I get nauseous just thinking about contending with it each day. Rather than offending him, I mentioned that I'm allergic to certain colognes and believe that the one he wears is on the list. Do you have any other suggestions for getting him to lighten up on his overpowering scents?

 Answer: If your co-worker does not get the hint, try seeing if you can get a cubicle transfer.

NAILS AND THEIR LENGTH

 Question: What do you consider to be a proper length for fingernails?

 Answer: Nails should be long enough to be able to catch a glimpse of them when you are looking at your hand with your palm towards you. Nails that are much longer begin to fall into the "claw" category.

A FEW WORDS ABOUT OUTERWEAR

Question: I need to buy a coat for work. However, I'm not sure what kind to get because I'll need to wear it with both my business professional and business casual clothes. Help!

Answer: You'll get the most mileage out of a trench coat with a zip out lining. Although studies have shown that a tan trench coat tests best in business, you certainly will be fine with one in black or navy.

BUTTONS

Question: What is the best way to recover from wearing clothes with a missing button?

Answer: That's something we all experience every now and again. Here are a few suggestions:

1. **Plan ahead.** Check your buttons as you lay your clothes out the night before. This way you can do something immediately if you find any loose buttons.
2. **Always leave home prepared.** Carry an emergency sewing kit with you that contains buttons and safety pins. If you find yourself in a pinch, you can be sure that a spare button (or pin) will be better than nothing at all.

GLOVES

Question: What kind of gloves should be worn in business?

Answer: Definitely wear a good pair of lined leather gloves. Choose the color based on your coat. If you are wearing a tan winter coat, brown leather gloves will work. If you are wearing a navy or black top coat, black leather gloves are more appropriate.

BRIEFCASES, SATCHELS, AND PURSES

Question: Five years ago, I would have never thought of leaving home without my purse. Today, I wonder if carrying one around—while also lugging around a computer case—looks too bulky. What do you think?

Answer: Carrying a purse that is small and functional is just fine. This way when you go to lunch, you can carry your essentials with you rather than lugging around the computer bag. However, be sure the purse you carry is a shoulder bag. Choose one that is large enough to be functional—yet small enough to comfortably wear over your shoulder.

THE PLACE FOR BACKPACKS

Q Question: I spent five years at a university carrying a backpack. Now that I've graduated from college and am in a career I love, I continue to carry a backpack for transporting paperwork to and from work. Is there a place for backpacks in the business arena?

A **Answer:** Thanks for asking. You've just described an often-made mistake made by recent graduates. While backpacks are functional, they are not appropriate in most professional business environments. The only exception would be if your organization makes them available to you with your company logo on them.

UMBRELLAS

Q Question: What type of umbrella should I have as part of my business wardrobe?

A **Answer:** Invest in an average-size black umbrella that is compact enough to be kept in your briefcase or computer bag. Depending on where you live and the season, you may not need an umbrella on a regular basis, but it's an accessory that you will want to have at your fingertips for both drizzles and downpours.

PUT A BRUSH TO THOSE SHOES

 Question: My dad always told me that customers can tell how well you take care of their projects by the way you maintain your shoes. Does this advice still hold true?

 Answer: Listen to your dad—he is absolutely right! In fact, many organizations place such a high value on well-polished shoes that they offer free shoe shines as part of a company perk. For instance, the Milwaukee-based law firm of von Briesen, Purtell, and Roper, S.C., have an arrangement with Mug N' Brush, a local shoe-shine shop. Each afternoon, a Mug N' Brush employee picks up shoes at the firm, polishes them, and returns them later that day.

SLIP-ON SHOE PROTECTORS

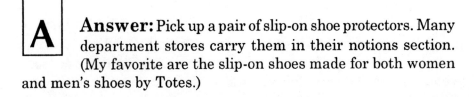 **Question:** How can I protect my shoes when it is raining or snowing without wearing boots?

Answer: Pick up a pair of slip-on shoe protectors. Many department stores carry them in their notions section. (My favorite are the slip-on shoes made for both women and men's shoes by Totes.)

CHAPTER 4

TIPS FOR MEN ON THE CLIMB

THE 9 MOST COMMON
DRESS MISTAKES MEN MAKE:

1. Wearing a dress shirt without an undershirt beneath it.
2. Not having custom-tailored shirts when it is difficult to find the proper fit.
3. Wearing a short-sleeved shirt beneath a blazer or suit jacket.
4. Wearing a tie that falls above or below the belt buckle rather than on it.
5. Flipping a tie over your shoulder when eating difficult-to-eat foods.
6. Not buttoning a sport coat or suit jacket when standing.
7. Not wearing socks that cover the calves.
8. Using a briefcase that is worn-looking.
9. Growing a goatee or beard when you have never seen top management with facial hair.

FACIAL HAIR

Question: What about facial hair for men?

Answer: The organization you represent should have a policy manual stating whether facial hair is acceptable. If nothing is stated on this subject, look around. Do men who have been promoted recently have facial hair? If so, does this facial hair consist of a mustache, goatee, or beard? If you find that any or all of the above are worn by men on the climb and upper-level male managers, go for it.

My only advice to you is to make the transition into facial hair when you are on a vacation. By growing out facial hair on your time, you will keep from looking scruffy on your company's time. Finally, once you have grown out the facial hair that works best for you and the organization you represent, be sure to keep it well maintained.

WHEN FACIAL HAIR SHOULD *NOT* BE WORN

Question: Is there ever a time when facial hair should *not* be worn?

Answer: The two times that facial hair should not be worn are:

1. When the upper-level male hierarchy in your organization does not have it.
2. When you are traveling to certain countries where it is not common for males to have facial hair (such as China).

WALLETS VS. MONEY CLIPS

Question: Which is preferred for men, using a money clip, carrying a wallet, or should both be carried?

Answer: It's a personal preference. A money clip works well for bills. Unless you keep your credit cards, driver's license, and other relevant documents in a planner or other type of carrier, you should also carry a wallet.

WATCHES

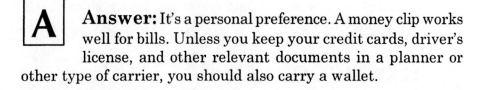

Question: What is considered proper business jewelry for men?

Answer: Whether you are dressed business professional or business casual, a dependable watch with a leather or metal band is in order. If you prefer to wear a watch that gives you more information than the time, be sure to shut it off. It is rather distracting when a watch beeps in the middle of a meeting.

OTHER JEWELRY IN THE WORKPLACE

Question: What other jewelry is considered appropriate for men in conservative environments?

Answer: When it comes to jewelry for men, wear no more than a watch, college class ring, and wedding band (if married).

JEWELRY TABOOS

Question: What isn't considered appropriate jewelry for men when at work?

Answer: Unless a man works in a creative environment and his male manager is into body piercing, keep earrings out of the workplace.

Look around to see what the higher-ups are wearing before you show up for work wearing necklaces or bracelets. If a ring is to be worn, it should be on the ring finger. Once again, in more creative environments, men may be able to wear a pinky ring.

COLOGNE: A LITTLE DAB 'ILL DO YA

 Question: Should cologne or aftershave be worn during the work day?

Answer: The issue about men wearing cologne is not *if* it should be worn but rather *how much* should be worn. The answer: A little dab 'ill do ya!

"**WHEN PUTTING ON COLOGNE, ALWAYS DO SO WITH YOUR LEFT RATHER THAN RIGHT HAND. IF YOU PUT COLOGNE ON WITH YOUR RIGHT HAND, ANYONE WHO SHAKES HANDS WITH YOU THAT DAY MAY EXPERIENCE THE AFTER EFFECTS OF YOUR COLOGNE.**"

—JIM ELLERS, GENERAL MANAGER, SEAGRAM AMERICAS

MANICURES

Question: Is it considered "prissy" for men to get manicures? My Dad always got them.

Answer: It sounds like your Dad was a terrific role model for you when it came to being well groomed. Like shoes, hands are a commonly noticed part of a person. By all means, invest in manicures on a regular basis.

UNDERSHIRTS AND DRESS SHIRTS
GO HAND IN HAND

Question: Is it really necessary for men to wear undershirts beneath dress shirts?

Answer: You bet. Here are the four benefits of wearing an undershirt beneath a dress shirt:

1. It keeps a starched shirt from itching.
2. When you perspire, an undershirt preserves your shirt.
3. It allows a white shirt to look even whiter.
4. It allows a dress shirt to lay better.

CREW NECK OR V-NECK?

Question: What kind of undershirts should be worn?

Answer: By all means, wear a v-neck undershirt. One of the most common undershirt faux pas that I see men make involves wearing a crew neck shirt beneath an open-collared dress shirt. While the layered look is fine for business casual days, don't allow your undershirt to show. It should *not* be considered part of a layered look.

WHAT ABOUT CHEST HAIR?

Question: Which is worse: having an undershirt show under an open-collared shirt or having chest hair show?

Answer: It's all in the mind of who has the chest hair and who is looking at the open-collared shirt. If you feel uncomfortable having your chest hair show, simply wear a crew neck undershirt beneath a buttoned open-collared shirt so that the undershirt doesn't show.

BUTTON DOWN
OR COLLAR WITH STAYS?

Question: Which are considered more formal: the button-down collar or the collar with stays?

Answer: While a button-down collar is certainly professional, it is one step less formal than a dress shirt that has a collar with stays. A button-down collar shirt works well with a sport coat and trousers.

When you are wearing a suit and would like to communicate a more conservative look, a white dress shirt that has a collar with stays should be your choice. When you are wearing a sport coat, however, and would like to communicate a look that falls between business professional and business casual, wear a sport coat with a button-down collar.

"THE RIGHT HON WAS A LITTLE TUBBY CHAP WHO LOOKED AS IF HE HAD BEEN POURED INTO HIS CLOTHES AND HAD FORGOTTEN TO SAY, 'WHEN!'"

—G. WODEHOUSE,
VERY GOOD, JEEVES (1930)

What about banded collars?

Question: As you know, in some parts of the country, banded collars are commonly worn under a sport coat. Are these shirts considered business casual or business professional items?

Answer: I'd put shirts with banded collars in the business casual category. They do not have the versatility of being worn with a tie.

Proper fitting dress shirts

Question: What is the proper fit for a dress shirt that is worn with a tie?

Answer: As far as the collar fitting properly, use the "one-finger test." When buying dress shirts, be sure that you can button the collar and still comfortably place your index finger between your neck and shirt collar. This fit will give you some breathing room and allow you to turn your neck without feeling as though you are wearing a straightjacket.

Short-sleeved shirts

Question: When is a short-sleeved collared dress shirt acceptable over a long-sleeved dress shirt?

Answer: In many organizations' business casual cultures, this type of short-sleeved collared shirt is appropriate all the time (such as warmer climates or when high-level management set the short-sleeve tone). However, they are not appropriate when wearing a sport coat or suit. In this case, a long-sleeved shirt should be worn.

A word about polo shirts

Question: What about polo shirts?

Answer: What about them? When wearing golf shirts, the most important rule is for the shirt to look fresh rather than unironed, crisp rather than worn and in a "business color" according to the organization you represent. If you are unsure of color, take a look at upper-level management and follow suit.

Note that some organizations prefer that their male employees wear button-down collared short-sleeved shirts rather than polo or golf shirts on business casual days.

Shirt and sleeve lengths

Question: How long should my shirt be and what length should my sleeves be?

Answer: Make sure the shirt is long enough to be tucked in without having to deal with a shirt tail. Your shirt sleeve should fall just a tad bit past your wrist bone. When you are wearing a jacket, the long-sleeved shirt should be approximately a half-inch longer than the sleeve of your jacket.

A word about cufflinks

Question: Are cufflinks a thing of the past?

Answer: It's a matter of personal preference. It is certainly a man's prerogative to wear cufflinks when his shirt has French cuffs and he is dressed professionally. The cufflinks themselves are considered an accessory and should be chosen in good taste. Make sure your cufflinks are either silver or gold (or that they give that appearance).

TIES

Question: Any tips for buying ties?

Answer: Invest in silk ties. This way you can be certain that they will tie well. Recognize that your tie is one of the ways to give your overall look an individual touch. If you prefer ties in a heavier quality fabric, wear them during the winter months.

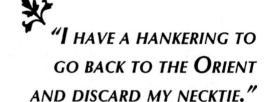

"I HAVE A HANKERING TO GO BACK TO THE ORIENT AND DISCARD MY NECKTIE."

—LIN YUTANG, WRITER/PHILOLOGIST

WHAT ABOUT TIE LENGTH?

Question: Where should my tie land on my body?

Answer: Be sure to invest in ties that are appropriate for your height. Once a tie is tied, it should touch the tip of your belt buckle.

Inappropriate ties?

Question: Are there certain types of ties that should not be worn?

Answer: Ties that are of poor quality or questionable taste (such as fish ties and the like) should be avoided. Also, when you are interacting with the British, be sure to avoid wearing a striped tie. The reason is that it could be similar to the person's regiment.

In addition, *never* wear a clip-on tie. This kind of tie is only appropriate for for security guards and individuals handling animals. Because it is so easy to take off, it may literally save their lives.

Tie widths

Question: What is an appropriate width for a tie?

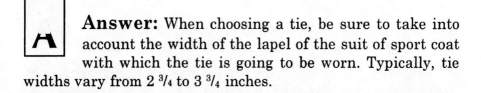

Answer: When choosing a tie, be sure to take into account the width of the lapel of the suit of sport coat with which the tie is going to be worn. Typically, tie widths vary from 2 ³/₄ to 3 ³/₄ inches.

TIE KNOTS

Q Question: Please discuss tie knots.

 Answer: When tying a tie, did you know that the smaller a knot, the more formal your look will be? Your three options for tying ties are the four-in-hand knot, the Windsor Knot, and the Half-Windsor Knot.

THE 6 STEPS FOR TYING A 4-IN-HAND KNOT

1. Begin with the wide end of the tie on your right, allowing it to hang approximately 12 inches below the narrow end.
2. Next, cross the wide end of the tie over the narrow part and then go back under the narrow part.
3. As you keep wrapping the tie around, be sure to move the wide end across the front of the narrow once again.
4. The next step is to pass the wide end of the tie through the loop.
5. As you hold the front of the knot loosely with your index finger, place the wide end down through the loop in the front.
6. Finally, tighten the knot. Take the tie up to the collar. Do so by holding the narrow end and sliding the knot up.

(Because the four-in-hand knot is long and straight, it usually works best with a standard shirt collar.)

THE 6 STEPS FOR TYING A WINDSOR KNOT

1. As with the four-in-hand knot, begin with the wide end of the tie on your right and extend it approximately 12 inches below the narrow end.
2. Cross the wide end over the narrow part and then up again on your right.
3. Next, take the wide end of the tie down around the narrow part and then up again on your right.
4. Place the tie first through the loop and then around across the narrow part.

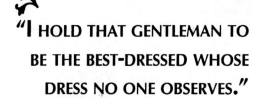

"I HOLD THAT GENTLEMAN TO BE THE BEST-DRESSED WHOSE DRESS NO ONE OBSERVES."

—ANTHONY TROLLOPE, ENGLISH NOVELIST, *THACKERAY*, 1879

5. Next, turn the tie and then take it up through the loop.
6. Finally, slip the tie through the knot in front. Tighten it and then draw it up snuggly to your collar.

(Because the Windsor Knot is wide and triangular, it usually works best with wide-spread shirt collars.)

THE 6 STEPS FOR TYING A HALF-WINDSOR KNOT

1. Begin with the wide end of your tie to your right and extend it 12 inches below the narrow end.
2. Cross the wide end of your tie up over the narrow end and then turn the tie back underneath.
3. Take your tie up and then turn it down through the loop.
4. Pass the wide end around the front of the tie from the left to the right.
5. Next, take your tie up through the loop.
6. Finally, take your tie down through the knot in front. Tighten your tie and then move it up to your collar.

(Because the Half-Windsor Knot is a medium symmetrical triangle, it usually works best with standard collars.)

POWER COLORS AND TIES

Question: What colors are considered power colors for ties?

Answer: If you want to project authority when wearing a tie, wear one that is predominantly red or yellow.

EATING WHILE WEARING A TIE

Question: In order to prevent food from being dropped on my tie, is it acceptable to tuck my tie between the first and second shirt button? Or would it be more appropriate to flip it over my shoulder?

Answer: The answer about what to do with ties when eating is simple: Be careful. The alternatives that you suggested are not acceptable options.

BOW TIES

Question: Should I wear a bow tie?

Answer: When dressed professionally, wearing a bow tie is a matter of choice. Individuals who represent organizations that encourage individual expression may do well wearing a bow tie. However, if you work for a company that has a fairly rigid dress culture, I'd stick with a regular tie.

JACKET STYLES

Question: What is the difference between an American-style jacket and a double-breasted one?

Answer: An American-style jacket has a single row of buttons; a double-breasted jacket has two rows of buttons.

BUTTONING A JACKET

 Question: When wearing a sport coat or suit jacket, when is it appropriate to button it?

 Answer: Any time a man stands, a sport coat or suit jacket should be buttoned. Besides the fact it is the appropriate thing to do, it shows that you pay attention to detail. It's one of those little things that makes a big difference.

WHICH BUTTONS?

 Question: Which buttons should be buttoned?

 Answer: When wearing either a sport coat or suit jacket, the following buttons should be fastened based on the style of the jacket:

◆ When wearing an American-style jacket with two buttons, the top button should be fastened when standing.

◆ When wearing an American-style jacket with three buttons, the top two buttons should be fastened when standing.

◆ When wearing an American-style jacket with four buttons, the first three buttons should be fastened.

◆ When wearing a double-breasted or European-style jacket, all the buttons should be fastened when standing.

WHAT IF I CAN'T BUTTON MY SUIT JACKET?

Question: What if I can't fasten my jacket buttons because it's too tight?

Answer: You have three choices: Lose weight, consult with a tailor about letting out the seams of the jacket, or buy a new one.

REMOVING JACKETS

Question: When wearing a sport coat or suit jacket, when should it be removed?

Answer: It may be removed either when those around you are not wearing one. Or if individuals around you are wearing jackets and invite you to remove your jacket, you may—if they also do. The only time I recommend that you leave your jacket on—even if others have removed theirs—is if you are delivering a presentation or want to project an authoritative image.

POCKET SCARVES

Question: How should I select a pocket scarf?

Answer: Typically, pocket scarves are worn in the after-five circles. The pocket scarf design should either be a color from the tie being worn or be in a print if a solid tie is being worn that evening. Some men play it safe by wearing a white pocket scarf.

The most important rule to follow when wearing a pocket scarf is to make sure it is compatible with the tie being worn rather than just having it look like a swatch of fabric from the tie.

ARE VESTS IN?

Question: What about wearing a vest?

Answer: While vests are viewed as one optional business accessory, they always add a touch of class to a professional wardrobe.

Ascots anyone?

Question: What are ascots and when may they be worn?

Answer: Ascots are small scarves that are more commonly worn by men outside the United States. An ascot is a small scarf made of silk or a similar material. It is placed around the neck beneath an open-collared shirt.

Pants: cuffs or no cuffs?

Question: What are the rules for wearing pants with cuffs?

Answer: While choosing to wear pants with cuffs is a personal choice, this touch gives a more formal look to trousers. In addition, it gives added weight to the pants.

If you do choose to wear a pair of pants with cuffs, be sure you are wearing them with a suit or other business professional attire. Otherwise, wearing a pair of slacks with plain bottoms is more appropriate. The only time cuffs are considered inappropriate is when wearing a tuxedo.

TROUSER LENGTHS

Question: Where should trousers break?

Answer: Trousers should break at the top of your shoes. Although many men may choose not to have the trousers break, the pant length should be long enough for the hem to skim the top of the shoe.

SUSPENDERS

Question: Should suspenders match your tie or your trousers?

Answer: Suspenders (also referred to as "braces") may match either. The most important thing to remember is to wear suspenders that button with the fasteners available in trousers specifically for this purpose. No clip-ons, please!

Belts or Braces

Question: Do belts and braces go hand in hand?

Answer: Either belts *or* braces should be worn—never both.

Belts

Question: My wife is always nagging me about the belts I wear. I am a conservative individual and feel that as long as I have a belt to match my shoes that's all that really matters. I have a brown belt, a black belt, and a maroon belt. I bought all of them a few years ago and intend to get my money's worth out of them. The big question is: How worn is too worn before a belt should be replaced?

Answer: If your wife tells you your belts need to be replaced, for goodness sake do it! Believe me, people in your private life are more apt to be candid with you than your manager (who may fear damaging your ego).

FILLING YOUR POCKETS

Question: How much is too much to put in trouser pockets?

Answer: Easy. If you have so much in your pocket(s) that it's apparent, take something out. The most important rule of thumb is to avoid clumps of keys, pockets full of change, and the like.

WHAT ABOUT SOCKS?

Question: Should socks match the shoes or trousers worn?

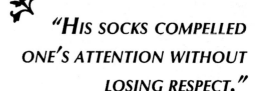

"HIS SOCKS COMPELLED ONE'S ATTENTION WITHOUT LOSING RESPECT."

—SAKI, *REGINALD*

Answer: The socks you choose should match either your trousers or shoes. For instance, when wearing navy trousers with black shoes, you may wear either black or navy socks. As for the style of sock, the dressier the sock, the more formal and lighter-weight your sock should be. When dressing business casual, a sock with a pattern is acceptable. Business casual attire also allows for a heavier sock. In either case, be sure to make sure your socks covers your calves.

Shoe style

 Question: When wearing a suit, what style of shoes should be worn? And what about when dressing in business casual attire?

 Answer: When wearing a suit, wing tip or oxford-style shoes should be worn to give the most professional look. On business casual days, the tassel loafer or oxford-style shoe works well. Whatever you do, avoid rubber-soled shoes.

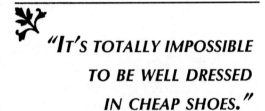

"It's totally impossible to be well dressed in cheap shoes."

—Hardy Amies, *The Englishman's Suit*, 1994

Color

 Question: What shoe colors should be worn with suits?

 Answer: When wearing business casual suits or trousers in black, navy, or charcoal, black shoes are best. When wearing a tan suit or khakis, cordovan or brown shoes work well.

WHAT YOUR SHOES SAY ABOUT YOU

Q Question: The organization I represent allows its employees to dress in both business casual and business professional attire. While I love having the flexibility, it's not all that easy when it comes to buying shoes. I don't want to wear my wing tips with casual clothes anymore than I feel as though my suede bucks are appropriate with suits. Help!

A **Answer:** First and foremost, invest in a pair of wing tips when wearing suits and a pair of leather slip-ons when dressing in business casual attire (such as dress pants along with an oxford open-collared shirt). Be sure to invest in shoes by purchasing the best you can afford. Finally, remember that buying good shoes is only half the job. Maintaining them is the key to demonstrating that you pay attention to detail.

Boots anyone?

Question: Where do boots fit in when dressing business casual?

Answer: Unless you live in the snowbelt during the winter, are in a fashion-forward field, live in the Southwest, or your CEO wears boots, save them for your personal time.

Briefcases

Question: Please address the styles and the use of briefcases.

Answer: When working in a conservative environment (such as a law firm), a leather briefcase may be the order of the day. However, if you are representing an organization that uses portable computers regularly, a canvas computer case that doubles as a carrier for documents or paperwork is typically used instead of a briefcase.

POWER PURCHASING POINTERS

Q Question: What are some general tips for men whose careers require them to dress in professional attire?

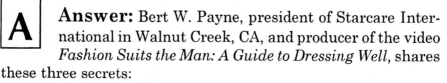

A **Answer:** Bert W. Payne, president of Starcare International in Walnut Creek, CA, and producer of the video *Fashion Suits the Man: A Guide to Dressing Well*, shares these three secrets:

1. **Be in the mood to shop when making a purchase.** Go to at least five men's stores before investing in a suit. Every retailer only carries selected styles. By taking the time to do your homework, you will become acquainted with the men's line that works best for you. This also will help you to invest in a suit that fits your body perfectly rather than buying one that requires extensive alterations.

2. **Coordinate, coordinate, coordinate.** When investing in a suit, select shirts, ties, and belts that will give your suit many different looks. Be sure to add accessories that will command presence by looking for pocket handkerchiefs, cufflinks, and socks.

3. **Think before you get your suits dry cleaned.** Suits should be dry cleaned infrequently. Frequent dry cleaning is hard on the interface, lining, and fabric of the suit. Instead, invest in a mahogany hanger (such as those carried by Neiman Marcus) and hang your trousers from the cuffs.

CHAPTER 5

TIPS FOR WOMEN CLIMBING THE LADDER OF SUCCESS

THE 8 MOST COMMON

DRESSING MISTAKES MADE BY WOMEN

1. Not wearing a blazer/suit jacket to meetings when the men present are dressed in suits or sport coats.
2. Having a hair style longer than shoulder length.
3. Carrying a purse that looks more like an overnight bag than something that simply holds a wallet, keys, makeup, etc.
4. Wearing hosiery that is darker than the skirt or pants being worn.
5. Wearing a skirt that is so short that it is distracting.
6. Wearing acrylic or fiberglass nails that look like claws.
7. Wearing an ankle bracelet in a business setting.
8. Wearing white shoes after Labor Day and before Memorial Day.

THE TAILORED LOOK WILL GET YOU AHEAD

Question: Why are tailored clothes considered to have that "business" look?

Answer: Tailored clothes are timeless and classic. They allow you to walk into *any* situation knowing that you will be wearing the right outfit. If you find that others are dressed more casually than you, tailored clothes allow you to remove a blazer and still be able to blend in to what others around you are wearing.

> *"FASHIONS FADE, STYLE IS ETERNAL."*
>
> —YVES SAINT LAURENT IN ANDY WARHOL'S INTERVIEW, NEW YORK (APRIL 13, 1975)

THE APPROPRIATE HAIR LENGTH FOR BUSINESS

Question: Does your hair length affect whether you are taken seriously?

Answer: You bet. Hair should be shoulder-length or shorter—or at least give that appearance. Otherwise, you may risk looking too much like a school girl.

How to dress conservatively
without giving up your femininity

Question: I work in a predominantly male company. What suggestions can you give me about dressing that will make me seen more as a *person* than as a *woman*?

Answer: The best advice I can give you is to wear tailored clothes. Make sure your jewelry is simple, yet elegant. Stay with solid colors or stripes rather than florals, lace, or gingham checks. The best way to know if a particular print is too feminine is to ask yourself if a man in your company would wear a tie with a comparable print.

A word about hair roots

Question: Is it acceptable to tell a colleague that she needs a root job? I have my roots done regularly while she waits too long between appointments to have hers taken care of.

Answer: If you know the person fairly well, simply mention how often you have your roots done in common conversation. If you don't know the person very well, mind your own roots!

PONYTAILS, PIGTAILS, AND SCRUNCHIES

Q Question: How do I politely tell a grown woman that ponytails and pigtails are not considered professional hairstyles in the workplace? Also, some women in our company pull up their hair with clips similar to the ones hair dressers use when cutting your hair. How can we discourage them from wearing these clips to work?

A **Answer:** Perhaps you can incorporate the standards expected in hair length and hair gismos into your organizations employee manual. Be sure you state that anyone choosing to have their hair shoulder length or longer should find a professional style for pulling it up (such as a chignon). State in your guidelines that ponytails or pigtails are considered more casual, rather than business professional (or even business casual).

Lastly, be sure to include scrunchies on your "inappropriate" list. Explain that while scrunchies may be good for pulling hair up and out of the way at home, they detract from even the best outfit.

"PREPPY CLOTHES ARE BUILT TO LAST, SINCE THEY WON'T GO OUT OF STYLE."

—LISA BIRNBACH,
THE OFFICIAL PREPPY HANDBOOK

GET OUT OF THE HABIT
OF TOUCHING YOUR HAIR

Question: Why do young women fresh out of school play with their hair so much?

Answer: Frequently, women fresh out of school have hair that is shoulder-length or longer. When this is the case, they tend to play it—a rather distracting habit that I'm sure they're unaware of.

Perhaps you can earmark this page and point this annoying habit out to them in this way. Otherwise, invite an image consultant to your company who may be able to integrate this distracting habit into his or her presentation.

DON'T COMB YOUR HAIR IN PUBLIC!

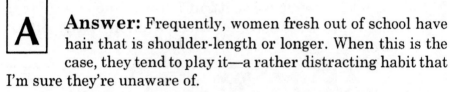

Question: Should combing your hair be saved for private moments? Or is it acceptable to run a quick brush or comb through one's hair when it appears that no one is around?

Answer: Combing hair, applying lipstick, and blowing one's nose should definitely be saved for private moments in private places—such as the bathroom! Anyone who is seen doing any of the above should be considered uncouth! Unfortunately the people who perform what seems to be these very harmless gestures don't have a clue that these things should be saved for restroom settings.

MAKEUP: TOO MUCH OR TOO LITTLE?

Question: Is it necessary to wear makeup to work? I never wear it but I sometimes wonder if I should because the other women in my office do.

Answer: Makeup is typically worn to enhance your features. While it certainly isn't necessary, it does add a bit of color to your face. Have you tried a touch of blush or perhaps lip gloss? These two items may do the trick without compromising your preference to not wear makeup.

"A WOMAN WHO DOESN'T WEAR LIPSTICK FEELS UNDRESSED IN PUBLIC. UNLESS SHE WORKS ON A FARM."

—MAX FACTOR, *TIME* (JUNE 16, 1958)

JEWELRY AND WORK

Question: Please address wearing jewelry in the workplace.

Answer: Jewelry should be worn as accessories for enhancing the clothes you wear to work. Wear enough jewelry to add that certain presence to your outfit, yet not so much that you look like you just left a gypsy camp.

When unsure if you are wearing too many pieces of jewelry with a given outfit, try following what I call "The Rule of 13." Count your pieces of jewelry. If you have more than 13 pieces on, you may be wearing a few too many.

"HAVE YOU EVER NOTICED, HARRY, THAT MANY JEWELS MAKE WOMEN LOOK FAT OR INCREDIBLY THIN?"

—J.M. BARRIE,
THE TWELVE-POUND LOOK AND OTHER PLAYS

While 13 may sound like a lot, it really isn't. Let's start counting: A pair of earrings (that's two), a necklace, watch, and two rings (we're up to five), a scarf and belt (eight) five gold-tones buttons on your jacket (bingo—that's 13). Case in point: Accessories on women really do add up fast.

PEARLS ANYONE?

Q Question: One of my favorite pieces of jewelry is my strand of cultured pearls. However, I see very few women wearing pearl necklaces today—especially among 20 to 30 year olds. Will I be perceived as outdated by wearing them?

A **Answer:** Perhaps you see pearls worn less today than in yesteryear because of the popularity of business casual dress in the workplace. While 14-karat gold and sterling silver can be worn with both business professional, business casual, and even casual attire, pearls should be saved exclusively for when you are wearing business professional clothes.

Note: When you are wearing cultured pearls, be sure to put them on *after* you have finished doing your makeup and hair. Makeup and the after-effects of spray, gel, etc. can be harmful to cultured pearls.

RINGS, RINGS,
AND MORE RINGS

Question: How many rings are too many? And on what fingers should they be worn?

Answer: In most work settings, a maximum of two rings should be worn, with no more than one on each hand. If you choose to wear a ring and are married, recognize that your engagement ring and wedding band count as one rather than two accessories because they are considered a set.

Because rings should be worn on either of your ring fingers (the one to the immediately left of your pinky) rings act as distractions when worn on a thumb, pinky, or center digit.

EARRINGS THE SIZE OF A QUARTER

Question: What is the absolute biggest an earring should be without jumping out at you?

Answer: It depends on the kind of work environment you represent. If you work in a professional atmosphere, I'd suggest wearing earrings that are no larger than the size of a quarter.

No matter what size earrings you decide are appropriate for you, be sure not to wear earrings that dangle so much that they can drag you down the corporate ladder!

WHAT ABOUT DOUBLE PIERCING?

Q Question: I've had my ears double-pierced for years. However, I have noticed that most of them women at my company only wear one earring in each ear. Do you think these women just don't wear more than one earring in each ear by choice or that this is a corporate culture thing?

A Answer: In most conservative and standard business cultures, wearing a maximum of one pair of earrings is considered acceptable. Wearing more than one pair gives a trendy appearance. Since the women in the company where you are employed appear to follow this standard, stick with wearing one pair.

Jewelry *NOT* to Wear to Work

Question: What kind of jewelry should not be worn to work?

Answer: Ankle bracelets, any piece of ostentatious jewelry, earrings larger than the size of a quarter, and dangling earrings should never be worn to the office.

Scarves

Question: What tips do you have when buying scarves? I love them on others yet don't seem to be able to wear them myself.

Answer: The next time you buy a scarf, invest in one made of silk. You will find that one made of silk will be easy to tie and will also lay well.

Also, the next time you see a woman wearing a scarf compliment her and then ask her how she drapes it. She'll probably be very flattered that you asked!

> *"We are all Adam's children but silk makes the difference."*
>
> —Thomas Fuller, *Gnomologia* (1732)

NAIL LENGTH

Question: What about nail length and the color of nail polish on women? Also, is it acceptable for women to wear fiberglass or acrylic nails?

Answer: The appropriateness of colored nail polish will vary based on the industry you represent. For instance, in more structured settings, (such as law firms, hospitals, and so forth), either clear polish or no polish at all would be a safer bet than gold glittered polish. At the same time, if you represent a more artsy culture, go for the more unusual colors, textures, and longer nail lengths.

A WORD

ABOUT UNDERGARMENTS

Question: What pearls of wisdom do you have when selecting undergarments?

Answer: I'll never forget a recent question that a soon-to-be female university graduate asked me at a seminar. She asked me if wearing a slip is considered old-fashioned.

A slip should be worn to either keep a top, skirt, or dress from clinging to the body. A slip is meant to give the garment form or to help preserve the outfit.

MINIMIZERS TO THE RESCUE

Question: I have a top-heavy figure which makes me very self-conscious. I rarely wear sweaters and tend to stay in a jacket at work. Is there a better way to appear less buxom?

Answer: Perhaps a minimizer (a bra specifically made to decrease your bust size) would help to make you feel less self-conscious.

WHICH OUTFITS PROJECT
THE MOST AUTHORITY?

Question: When dressing in business professional attire, what kind of clothes tend to project the most authority for women?

Answer: Here's a list of four outfits rated from highest to lowest on how they project authority:

1. A skirted suit.
2. A blazer and contrasting jacket and skirt.
3. A dress.
4. A jacket and tailored trousers.

WHAT ABOUT A SLACKS SUIT?

Q Question: As a new associate in a very conservative law firm, I have been wearing skirted suits to work. I feel more comfortable, however, in slacks suits. While there are no women at a higher level in our department whose dress I can mimic, my male manager dresses to the nines (cufflinks and all). Would I be out of place wearing a conservative slacks suit to work?

A Answer: Based on what you shared with me, I'd stick with a skirted suit. However, if and when you see your impeccably dressed manager wearing a sport coat and trousers rather than a suit, it will be your cue to also "kick down your dress a notch" with a tailored slacks suit.

Blouses

Question: What advice do you have about choosing blouses for business?

Answer: Avoid blouses that are too low or too sheer. As far as color, recognize that a blouse can make or break a basic outfit. When wearing a blazer with a pair of tailored slacks or a skirt, a blouse that is darker than the jacket itself will lend an authoritative presence to your overall look. Also, be sure to wear blouses that are made of a fabric compatible with the rest of your outfit. Whatever you do, avoid wearing blouses with gingham checks, lacy collars, and flowery prints on them.

Skirt lengths:
The 8½" x 11" rule

Question: What is considered the proper skirt length for women?

Answer: When it comes to skirt length, women have a few options. When working in a conservative setting, a skirt that is two to three inches above the knee is

TEXAS STATE TECH. COLLEGE
LIBRARY-SWEETWATER TX.

considered appropriate. In a very creative and fashion-forward environment, women may be able to get away with wearing skirts that are shorter in length. Ankle-length skirts are also in style today.

In any case, the most important tip I can give women regarding skirt length rule is the 8½" x 11" rule. Sit down, take an 8½" x 11" piece of paper, and place it on your lap. Your skirt cover the same amount of length as the paper.

WHAT YOUR SKIRT LENGTH SAYS ABOUT YOU

Q **Question: Does it really matter what skirt length I choose to wear?**

Answer: Choosing your skirt length is really up to you. However, keep this in mind: Skirts that are "too" short and those that fall to the ankle is perceived to be more "trendy" where skirt lengths that are within a few inches of your knee are more "traditional."

How to be sure your skirt length is fashionable without being distracting

Question: When choosing my skirt length, what should I consider?

Answer: Your safest bet is to consider the business climate where you will be. If you will be in a more conservative environment, you may want to choose a skirt that is within a few inches of the knee. If you are in a more relaxed environment, a longer skirt or even tailored slacks may work better.

Tips for minimizing your thighs

Question: I have inherited larger legs. What can I do to play them down?

Answer: You are living in the right time because there are several options from which to choose. For example, by wearing plain dark-colored tailored slacks, you will play down your thighs rather than accentuating them. Add an over-the-hip jacket, matching jacket, and bright-colored blouse to these clothes and you're ready to go.

If you see that your waist is one of your assets, accentuate it by wearing a belt that matches your jacket and tailored slacks or skirt. Also, by wearing dark hosiery and shoes that match your slacks or suit, you will give yourself a finished look.

When you do choose to wear skirts, either choose those with a flair that fall within a few inches of your knee. You also have the option of wearing skirts that fall to the middle of your calves.

DECORATIVE BELTS

Q Question: As a business woman, is it appropriate to wear anything other than a quality leather belt? Are decorative belts (gold and silver chain belts, seasonal belts, belts with imprints, etc.) considered unprofessional?

A Answer: It really depends on the dress culture of your organization. Decorative belts may be fine within organizations that do not have a stringent dress code. They also may be fine on business casual day.

However, your best bet for knowing what's appropriate is by mirroring the highest-level woman in your organization. Most likely, she has risen to the top due to her capabilities and also because she looked the part of an executive.

What happened to skirts?

Q Question: Have skirts been left in the last century? It seems to me that the only company that would expect its female employees to wear skirts would be the ones stuck in the 20th century.

A **Answer:** Although tailored slacks suits have replaced skirted suits, suits with skirts are still worn on a regular basis by women in very conservative work environments. Today, the skirts that are worn tend to be in varying lengths from a few inches above the knee to midcalf and even slightly longer.

Fabrics that are

less than businesslike

Q Question: What fabrics do you believe should be kept out of the work environment?

 Answer: Leather, fleece, denim, crepe, satin, and velvet are a few fabrics to avoid wearing in business professional environments. While leather and denim may be acceptable in selected environments, they give a very casual appearance. Clothes made of crepe, satin, and velvet should be saved for evening wear. Clothes made of fleece should be left for weekend wear.

APPROPRIATE SKIRT LENGTHS

Question: As I look around the office, it seems that women's skirts are getting shorter and shorter. Is there an "appropriate" skirt length in a professional setting?

Answer: If you think your skirt is too short, it probably is! Typically, skirts should be no shorter than one to three inches above the knee.

When an employee's skirt is too short

Question: As a male manager, what is the best way to approach one of my female employees whose skirt is too short?

Answer: You have a few choices. If you have a written dress code that states the suggested skirt length for women, ask this person to refer to her employee manual. Otherwise, if you have a female human resource director, I recommend that you ask her to speak to the person. (If you do not have a female H.R. director, ask one of your female counterparts to speak with the person.) Whatever you do, tread these waters lightly. Don't set yourself up for a potential sexual harassment suit.

That little black dress

Question: I work in the dress department of a major department store. A customer came in and asked me to help her find "a little black dress." I didn't know what to get for her. What is "a little black dress?"

Answer: Every woman should have a basic black dress. While the style can vary based on body shape, this dress makes a statement, while still giving a timeless and understated look. However, the fabric and style of the dress should transcend all occasions. This can be done by dressing it up with accessories (such as jewelry, scarves, jackets, etc.). Because of its versatility, a little black dress is incredibly useful when travelling. If you're having difficulty finding a little black dress, consider contacting travelsmith.com. Travelsmith.com is a catalog company that carries a wide variety of little black dresses.

A WORD ABOUT DRESSES

Question: When dressing in business professional attire, does wearing a dress command the same presence as a suit?

Answer: A tailored dress with a matching jacket can command as much presence as a skirt suit. The key is to be sure to accessorize the dress with jewelry, a scarf, and/or pumps to give it that professional look.

The ABCs of maternity dress

Question: I'm three months pregnant and feel my clothes getting snug. What do you suggest I wear to work without looking frumpy?

Answer: Today, there are great clothes for the expectant mother. If you haven't done so already, be sure to always take female friends (who are your size) up on their offer to loan you their maternity clothes to you. It will save you a lot of money.

Browse around maternity shops to see what's out there. Also, take a look around clothing consignment stores for a maternity section. Buy the basics that will take you through your pregnancy (such as black slacks, skirts, etc.). Be sure that the items you purchase can be mixed and matched with at least two other garments in your new wardrobe. Finally, keep your clothes interesting by adding scarves and jewelry.

Dress tips for the menopausal woman

Question: What dress advice do you have for women experiencing hot flashes?

Answer: If you haven't figured it out already, dressing in layers is definitely the way to go when you are in the throes of hot flashes. A blouse, sweater, and jacket may be perfect for those cold and blustery winter days. However, when you feel a flash approaching, you can nonchalantly remove your blazer (and perhaps even your sweater) allowing yourself to cool down.

Shoes for all seasons

Question: Does the rule about only wearing white shoes after Memorial Day and until Labor Day still apply?

Answer: You bet. In fact, a commonly made shoe faux pas that women make is wearing white shoes before and after these days. Another mistake that women who don't know better make involves wearing suede shoes in the spring or summer. Suede shoes should be worn only in the late fall and winter.

If the shoe style fits, wear it!

Question: Are there any shoes that are not appropriate for the workday?

Answer: In most business environments, sandals aren't considered appropriate for the workplace. Also, shoes made from peau de soie are better suited for that next formal gathering or wedding you'll attend rather than for work.

Heels: How high is *too* high?

Question: How many inches should the heel of a shoe be?

Answer: Typically, a heel should be two to three inches high. Go much higher and you may look like you are walking on stilts. However, if you are in the fashion industry, you will be able to get away with a higher heel. At the same time, if you are in a role where you are on your feet a lot, a shoe with a flat heel rather than a raised one may be more practical.

When you are tall

Question: As a tall woman, I often find myself towering over men. Is it acceptable to wear flats with business professional attire?

Answer: Several years ago, a six-foot-tall female client of mine explained what happened when she wore flats with a suit. She was meeting with male clients who happened to be considerably shorter than her. However, one client recognized that she made a point of wearing flats. This was a silent cue to him that she was overly conscious of his height. He told her that he would prefer she wear heels than modify the height of her shoes to accommodate his stature.

OPEN-TOE VS. CLOSED-TOE SHOES

Question: There are so many styles of shoes to choose from. Which style is best for the workplace?

Answer: Whether you are dressed business professional or business casual, a closed-toe shoe in a high-quality leather is the best choice for the workplace.

TENNIS SHOES

Question: I frequently park a few blocks from my building and then walk to my office. During the workday, it's common for me to attend meetings that are only a few blocks away. What's your take on athletic shoes?

Answer: While I totally agree that it is important to wear extremely comfortable shoes when walking short distances, wearing athletic shoes to work is for women no better than a man wearing slippers with his suit. Flats with rubber soles are comfortable, and certainly look better than athletic shoes with work clothes. Espirit makes a great line of shoes that fit the bill.

SHOE COVERINGS

Question: What kind of foot covering can you recommend for inclement weather?

Answer: Rubber overshoes are a definite must for days of torrential rain and light snow. Otherwise, a pair of boots that can be worn to and from work are a must. I suggest black because it goes with everything.

HOSIERY

Question: How do you know what color of hosiery to wear?

Answer: Easy. When wearing hosiery, be sure to select a shade that is the same or lighter than your skirt or pants hem. For instance, if you are wearing a black skirt or slacks, you may wear hosiery in a "barely black" or "nude" tone. If you are wearing a beige skirt, hosiery in a nude or ivory tone is appropriate.

A commonly-made faux pas women make is wearing dark hosiery with a short-sleeved outfit. The guideline to be followed is this: If part of your forearm and elbow to wrist are showing, skin-toned hosiery should be worn.

Finally, always keep a pair of skin-toned hosiery with you at the office. If you have a spare pair nearby and find you have a run, it will allow you to keep your professional look intact without having to go to the closest store to purchase another pair.

WHAT ABOUT TROUSER SOCKS?

Question: When dressing business casual, are trouser socks for women acceptable?

Answer: Trouser socks are appropriate based on the style of shoe worn. For instance, if a loafer, an oxford-style shoe, or a shoe that ties is worn, trouser socks work well.

MULES

Question: What are the rules with mules?

Answer: Mules (shoes with an open back) are considered more casual than business casual. Save them for when you are on your own time rather than wearing them to work.

How large should my purse be?

Question: I am attending college and interning for a company where I hope to begin my career. While in the office, I have noticed the variety of purses women carry to work. They range from small handbags to overflowing totebags. Is there an unspoken rule concerning the size and type of purse a woman takes to work?

Answer: Good question. The purse you carry should be large enough to be functional. The most practical ones for work are "Coach-like" leather shoulder bags.

What color
should my purse be?

Question: I had heard that a woman's purse should be color-coordinated with her shoes. Is this really necessary?

Answer: A purse should be the same color as your shoes. However, as you are building your wardrobe, it may not be practical to have a purse for each pair of shoes you own. When this is the case, stick with black which will work when you are wearing navy blue or brown shoes.

CHAPTER 6

MUCH ADO ABOUT NOTHING?

THE 6 MOST COMMON
BUSINESS CASUAL MISTAKES

1. Misinterpreting "casual" clothes as business-casual attire.
2. Not recognizing that the *real* definition of most business casual dress codes is dressing one notch down.
3. Believing that the term "permanent press" means that clothes don't need to be pressed or even touched up with an iron.
4. Not paying the same attention to shoes when dressing business casual that you do when dressing business professional.
5. Wearing business casual attire on dress down days without having an "emergency" suit at work for that unexpected meeting.
6. Wearing shirts out of your pants rather than tucking them in.

THE PROS AND CONS
OF GOING BUSINESS CASUAL

Question: What kind of studies have been conducted regarding the advantages and disadvantages of companies relaxing their dress codes?

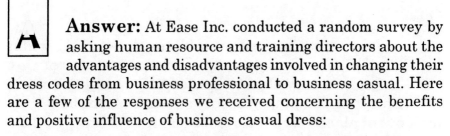

Answer: At Ease Inc. conducted a random survey by asking human resource and training directors about the advantages and disadvantages involved in changing their dress codes from business professional to business casual. Here are a few of the responses we received concerning the benefits and positive influence of business casual dress:

More relaxed, feeling of choice, use of judgment, and more personal control.

A "free" additional benefit to our employees.

Clothing is less costly for employees.

It tends to help perceptions of senior management as being "real" people which fosters teamwork.

Employees work better when they are more comfortable.

Increases comfort, workers fit in better with customers and appear more approachable.

When asked about the disadvantages of making the transition to business casual, approximately 20 percent of the human resource and training directors who responded indicated that employee productivity as a whole had decreased. Based on the responses, they felt that dressing down:

Lowered productivity.

Was too casual—caused a casual work ethic.

◆ Created an atmosphere of extreme familiarity that brought on unprofessional behavior.

◆ Lowered productivity on Fridays.

◆ Encouraged a more relaxed work environment. As a result, many employees acted less formal and considerate.

◆ Caused staff to act more relaxed and casual (less professional) thus not helping them to distinguish between their roles at home and the office.

DRESS CODES EXIST TO BE FOLLOWED

Q Question: Can you ever be *too* dressed up when others are dressed in business casual attire? Our firm is a very old and conservative establishment. While most of the young associates feel as though they look out of place, our senior partners insist that we abide by the business professional dress code.

A Answer: I understand what you are saying. Conservative dress and business casual are at such opposite ends of the spectrum that even many law firms are questioning the value of suits. In one instance, when showing up in suits for a client meeting where everyone else was wearing business casual attire, one group of young lawyers said they felt as though they looked more like undertakers than legal counselors.

However, no matter how "stuffy" you may feel wearing a suit, the bottom line is that an organization's dress standards were created to be followed.

WHY ARE THERE 2 SCHOOLS OF THOUGHT ABOUT BUSINESS CASUAL?

Q Question: I don't get it. So many companies have instituted business casual as a "perk" and see it as working well for their organizations. Others believe that employees who wear casual clothes begin to act too relaxed. Why are there such varying responses?

A **Answer:** Good question. It's hard to understand why the switch to business casual dress can result in an increase in productivity for some companies, while it is perceived as decreasing productivity for others. Many of us are familiar with the popular saying "Image is everything." I don't agree with the severity of this statement, yet I do believe image counts for something. When you feel confident about the way you look, you will usually convey that confidence. When you feel neatly arranged, together, organized, and professional, you will tend to perform in such a manner. Even Micah, my six-year-old miniature schnauzer appears to live by this rule. After Micah returns from the groomer, look out! It's obvious by the way he prances down the street and throws around his weight (about 15 pounds) that the way he looks affects the way he acts...even if he is a pooch!

DRESSING DOWN CAN GIVE A PROFESSIONAL PRESENCE

Question: Is it still possible to project a professional presence when wearing business casual clothes?

Answer: You bet. Even when you are dressed down, you can still maintain your professional demeanor. Keep in mind that business casual dress is different than dressing in a haphazard manner that turns heads for the wrong reason. This may ultimately have a negative effect on your work ethic.

SATURDAY ATTIRE

Question: When you go to the office on Saturday mornings to catch up on work, how "low" can you go? I've seen some employees show up in shorts, jeans, and jogging suits.

Answer: The only hard-and-fast rule you should follow is to emulate the highest-level person's Saturday dress. In other words, if you've seen your company's CEO wearing an open-collar shirt and slacks on Saturday, emulate that person. I assure you that by wearing politically correct clothes on Saturdays, you will be noticed.

SETTING THE BUSINESS CASUAL STAGE

Question: When it comes to instituting a company image, what role should employers play?

Answer: One of the most common mistakes made by employers when implementing business casual is the direction and structure they fail to provide. Employers: Never assume your employees know what appropriate business casual dress entails. True, the majority of individuals do know what's appropriate for business casual attire, yet there are always a few unenlightened apples.

TALK ABOUT A JUGGLING ACT!

Question: As a woman, I find it very difficult to balance the newest fashion trends and an "I-mean-business" appearance. It seems that women's clothing is evolving toward shorter and tighter fit, including business suits. I can recognize when clothes are too short for a professional environment, yet cannot seem to differentiate when something is too tight! What should I do?

Answer: When trying clothes on, if it even crosses your mind that they are too tight, you're probably right. Simply follow the rule: When in doubt, don't wear it!

BUSINESS CASUAL SHOE STYLE

Question: What shoes are business casual?

Answer: For women, a shoe that is a cross between a pump and a loafer with a chunky heel is frequently a good choice. Typically, summer sandals and work environments do not go hand in hand with business casual. As for men, slip-on or oxford-style shoes are recommended for those dress-down days.

MAKING THE TRANSITION

Question: The company I work for recently made the transition from business professional to business casual. It is great to be comfortable at work, however I am a bit distressed. Because we do not have a written policy for business casual, it is hard to determine what is acceptable. When I dressed business professional every morning, it was a "no-brainer"; I chose the suit and tie I wished to wear. Now that we've gone business casual, I find myself wondering if the outfits I choose are appropriate to wear to work.

Answer: My first suggestion to you would be to mirror your manager, upper-level executives, and those who are successfully climbing the ladder of success. Take note of how these individuals dress—these are the people who will set the dress standard within your company, especially since you don't have a written dress code.

I also encourage you not to let business casual dress turn into "casually sloppy" dress. Pay attention to detail. Employees often fail to do this when dressing business casual. Just because your dressing on the casual side doesn't mean it's acceptable to wear wrinkled clothes, scuffed shoes, or clothing that may appear worn.

As far as specifics dealing with what you should or shouldn't wear, this depends mostly on your corporate culture. Below are some examples of some typical "no-nos" listed in many business casual dress policies.

The following is a list of what many companies consider business casual dress blunders:

Denim (jeans, skirts, jumpers, shirts, bib overalls, blue or colored denim, etc.).
Leather.
Sweatpants.
Sweatshirts.
Work-out or jogging outfits.
Shorts.
T-shirts.
Sleeveless tops without a jacket or sweater.
Clothing with extreme or outrageous colors.
Uncoordinated clothing and color combinations.
Revealing or transparent items.
Baggy or sloppy-looking sweaters.
Wrinkled clothing.
Shoes that appear to be worn or unkempt.
Athletic shoes.
Thong-type sandals.
Women failing to wear hosiery or socks.

Men wearing shoes without socks.

Baseball caps.

Polo shirts with sport logos.

Wearing pants without a belt.

Shirts without collars.

Tops with plunging necklines.

Dresses or tops with spaghetti straps or exposed shoulders.

Short skirts or dresses.

TAMING THE PREDICTABLE

Q **Question: Our company is very slow to make changes. They are finally instituting business casual dress on an everyday basis. However, I've heard that when given this privilege, employees often misinterpret casual clothes for business casual attire (such as stretch pants, sandals, concert T-shirts, etc.). As the human resource director, how do I keep this from happening in our company?**

A **Answer:** If your company is going business casual, be sure to provide a written set of dress standards before it is made effective. Specify in detail what your company defines as appropriate dress-down attire and what is considered *too* casual.

Many companies that have implemented business casual dress give examples of what is considered an appropriate combination. For example, you may want to set the example of appropriate attire to be khakis and polo with your company's logo, or a shirt with a collar, sweater, and khakis. You may want to list that appropriate attire for women means tailored slacks, a skirt that is a few inches within the knee or closer to the ankles.

By providing employees with specific options, you will be defining the dress standards, while leaving room for comfort and individuality. Recognize that productivity is affected and influenced at both the wide and narrow level. Even if individuals feel confident about the way they look, the environment that surrounds them can still have a significant influence. If a few individuals appear unprofessional and unproductive, it can drastically effect the whole.

WHY DEFINING A BUSINESS CASUAL DRESS CODE IS IMPORTANT

Q **Question: I believe that our employees have good taste. As we are going to business casual, I feel as though it will insult the intelligence of our team by putting a dress code in writing.**

A **Answer:** No matter how tastefully your team dresses on business professional days, you can beed assured that the company switch to business casual and all it entails can backfire.

Most companies hope that business casual will help them fit in with their surrounding business communities, encourage a more unified work environment, and provide comfort. In order for this to be accomplished, business casual dress must first be defined by the employer. I can't tell you how many questions and inquiries our company receives concerning business casual dress. The majority of these inquiries can be summed up in one major question: "What *is* business casual?"

Many individuals wake up each morning not only wondering what to wear, but if it's even appropriate! Questions that cross many women's minds are "Is it all right to wear open-toed shoes?" "Is hosiery a necessary evil?" "How short is *too* short for a dress?" "Are Doc Martin's acceptable?" "Are cargo pants considered khakis?" "What about a denim shirt?"

If you don't already have a business casual dress code, look at the sample dress codes on pages 197-199.

CREATING STANDARDS
FOR BUSINESS CASUAL

Question: What are some do's and don'ts about dressing business casual when a firm does not have a written dress code?

Answer: Angela Hazlett, an account executive with a public relations firm, shares these do's and don'ts from both observations and experience:

1. Never wear torn or stained clothing, scuffed shoes, or hosiery with runs. Keep a pair of extra hosiery, a small mending kit, and instant cleaning wipes at your desk for those unexpected spills.

2. Keep nails and hair neatly groomed. Be sure to keep a hairbrush or comb with you. Also, if you're going to use nail polish, consider a clear or a sheer nail polish.

3. Sweatshirts or fabric made for jogging pants is unacceptable for office settings—even on business casual Fridays.

4. Try wearing a dressy pair of pants with a casual garment on dress-down Fridays. For instance, wear dress
   pants with a nice sweater.
5. I never wear athletic shoes to work—even on the most
   casual of dress-down days.

THE DISADVANTAGES OF WEARING

BUSINESS CASUAL CLOTHES

Q **Question:** My company has recently changed over
to business casual attire. As the company's owner
I've wasted more time each morning trying to
decide what to wear since I realize that the way I dress
sets the expectations I have for my employees. When
dressing business professional, it was a no-brainer. I'd
just put on a suit and march out the door. Wearing
business casual, however, takes a lot more thought.

A **Answer:** You're not alone. Like you, many individuals have shared that although they enjoy the comfort of
business casual, they miss the simplicity of business professional. When dressing business professional, they felt confident about what to wear each day.

Besides saving yourself a lot of time each morning, by providing the structure of an acceptable and specific policy, you will
ease the minds of your staff, encourage confidence, and promote
productivity by showing them what you expect.

BUSINESS CASUAL

CAN LEAD TO BUSINESS SLOPPY

Q Question: During a recent performance appraisal, my manager told me that my definition of business casual was not what she considered businesslike. She felt that I looked disheveled on business casual days and encouraged me to pay more attention to the way my clothes were maintained. What should I do?

A **Answer:** Too often, if given enough time, individuals dress as if they believe business casual really means "casual sloppy." Many times without realizing it, people take the path of least resistance when it comes to dressing—especially on business casual days. In time business casual can lead to casually sloppy, which can lead to a casual work ethic.

By the mere fact that you are sharing your manager's constructive criticism with me, it's apparent that you want to project an "I-mean-business" attitude. My advice to you is to make a concerted effort to pay attention to the little things. Be sure your clothes are pressed, all the buttons are on your shirts, your shoes are polished, your hair and nails are clean, and you shower at the start of the day. By doing these little things, you will show that you mean business—even on dress-down days. You also will be communicating that added confidence, status, and work ethic to your manager and to those around you.

Below are seven tips for showing that you mean business by the way you dress:

1. Go beyond business casual by dressing one notch up from what is expected. If you have your eye on a higher position, the trick is to dress as though you already have the position. Dress with status in mind.

2. Mirror your manager and other upper-level executives. The way they dress will help you to recognize your organization's dress culture.

3. Pay attention to detail. Detail will differentiate you from the rest of your colleagues. Always iron your clothes. Be sure to wear a nice belt and polish your shoes, even when dressing business casual.

4. Avoid wearing clothes that appear worn and make sure that your clothes are a good fit.

5. Make sure your pants are the proper length.

6. Grooming is an important factor. Often, men assume they can slip by without shaving on dress-down days. Don't do it!

7. Likewise, women should make a point of styling their hair on dress-down days instead of pulling their hair up with a scrunchie.

WHEN BUSINESS CASUAL
SHOULD *NOT* BE WORN

Question: Now that business casual dress is the rule rather than the exception in most companies, I must ask, when should it *not* be worn?

Answer: Below are 10 times to kick your dress into a business professional mode:

1. When out-of-town clients are visiting your organization and you're not sure how they will be dressed.
2. When visiting a client's site for the first time and are unsure of their dress code.
3. When you are giving a presentation to a client.
4. When interviewing new employees.
5. When a performance appraisal is taking place.
6. When participating in a meal at a formal restaurant with a client.
7. When interacting with international clients.
8. During a company's board of directors' meeting.
9. When interacting with governmental agencies.
10. When your company is being audited.

WHEN EMPLOYEES SHOW UP

FOR WORK DRESSED INAPPROPRIATELY

Q **Question: It was a good idea at the time. When our company decided to go business casual, we considered it to be a company perk. However, the** way some of our employees show up dressed for work is out of control. What is the best way to approach the subject with an employee without demotivating him or her for the rest of the day?

A **Answer:** Business casual is only as good as the organization's dress code guidelines that go with it, along with the managers or human resource directors who make sure it is followed.

When a person is dressed inappropriately for your organization's dress culture, I recommend that you speak immediately with that person. Make a copy of the guidelines available. Make sure the person is not going to have direct customer contact that day. If so, send the person home to change—on his or her own time. By taking these measures, you will be setting a precedent for both that person and anyone else who may not have realized that dress code guidelines are written to be followed.

WILL BUSINESS CASUAL
BE A THING OF THE PAST?

Q Question: Where do you see business casual going? I've worked for the same company for five years. In that short period of time, our dress standards have gone downhill. It's to the point that our own employees comment about how one person or the other shows up dressed for work. Unfortunately, these individuals' managers look as bad as their employees. Please give me your opinion on where dress will go during the next few years.

A Answer: What people wear to work has definitely deteriorated during the 1990s and it sounds like your organization's employees may be an example of this. The "Give an inch, take a mile" rule is reflective in today's business casual dress in many organizations. I genuinely believe that everything goes full circle...including dress.

A perfect example is one company on the West coast that was so tired of individuals "dressing down" that they instituted each Monday as "Dress-up Day."

Because business casual began as a perk at many companies, the only way I see the pendulum swinging back to "dressing up" is if it is posed to employees as a benefit (for example, the company purchasing blazers and slacks for anyone who chooses to dress up wearing these clothes).

CHAPTER 7

DRESSING FOR JOB INTERVIEWS

 THE 6 MOST COMMON
INTERVIEW DRESSING MISTAKES

1. Not recognizing that body piercing is offensive to many interviewers.
2. Erring on the conservative side when you're not sure of a company's dress policy.
3. Wearing a skirted suit rather than a slacks suit to a first interview when you're not sure how women in comparable positions dress.
4. Not recognizing that you can change the look of the suit you wore to the first interview by wearing another shirt, tie, etc.
5. Dressing less formally after you land a job than you did when you interviewed for the position.
6. Dressing for the position you have rather than the one you want.

Body piercing and job interviews

Q Question: I am working on my college degree at a liberal arts college. It is the norm rather than the exception for everyone to have his or her body pierced in several places (ear, eyebrow, nose, and tongue, just to name a few). Because I will be applying for an internship position this summer, I want to know what is considered appropriate. Help!

A Answer:
Depending on where you will be applying for internships, I'd suggest only wearing one pair of earrings. Leave the jewels for your brow, nose, and tongue on campus because they may be a deterrent rather than an enhancement to the impression you make at the interview.

Frequently, recruiters interpret what you wear to an interview as what you will be wearing to work if they choose to hire you—and that includes all of your accessories.

"I'VE REALLY TRIED TO LEARN THE ART OF CLOTHES BECAUSE YOU DON'T SELL FOR WHAT YOU'RE WORTH UNLESS YOU LOOK GOOD."

—Lady Bird Johnson

WHAT TO WEAR TO AN INTERVIEW

Q Question: I have an upcoming interview for an internship position with a potential employer and I have a few questions. Because the job I am interviewing for would involve laboratory work, should I wear business attire or laboratory attire to the interview? I want to make a good impression with my interviewer and am not sure if I should just go ahead and dress up, or if that would be overstepping my boundaries from laboratory rat to business executive?

A **Answer:** Definitely dress up. You can never get in trouble looking good. As great as it would be to be part of the company, keep in mind that you are interviewing them as much as they are interviewing you. For that reason, put your best self forward by wearing a sport coat and trousers or a suit—whichever one you own that you feel the best wearing. Be sure your shoes are "spiffed-up" so that the interviewer knows you pay attention to detail.

Once you land this position—or whatever one you are ultimately meant to have—remember to always dress like an individual on the climb rather than your colleagues. You'll be promoted much quicker.

A SKIRT OR SLACKS?

Q Question: I am interviewing for an associate position with a banking institution. I plan to dress in business professional style for the interview...but does that mean I have to wear a skirt? Wouldn't a nice pants suit be just as professional?

A **Answer:** While a slacks suit would be semi-professional, because your interview is with a banking institution, I'd definitely show up at the first interview dressed in a skirted suit. While you're at the interview, notice how the women who are in professional roles are dressed. This will give you a clue about wearing a slacks suit to that second or third interview. Finally, you also may want to ask about dress guidelines during the interview itself.

2 INTERVIEWS BACK TO BACK

Q Question: I have two job interviews on the same day. One company has a business casual policy while the other dresses business professional. I'm not quite sure how to dress for the day considering that I won't have time to return home to change. Help!

 A **Answer:** Rule number one: You cannot get in trouble looking good. I'd suggest that you put your most professional self forward by slipping into your business suit at the start of the day. Although the first company you mention has a business casual policy, you may be surprised to learn that their CEO may wear a sport coat or suit. This inconsistency in dress is usually from high-power meetings outside their office in which business professional dress may be more appropriate.

WHEN YOU ONLY OWN
ONE INTERVIEW OUTFIT

Q Question: I am preparing to go to a second interview for a job that I'd really like to be offered. Because I will not be graduating from college for a few months, I only own one decent pair of interview slacks along with a blazer, which I've already worn to the first interview. Will I sabotage my chances for being offered the position by wearing the same outfit to the second interview?

A Answer: Not at all. Wear the same slacks and blazer, changing the shirt or tie (if you are a man) or the scarf and earrings (if you are a woman). Most interviewers will not be distracted if you show up in the same outfit. However, if your clothes are not well maintained they will probably notice.

INTERVIEW ATTIRE FOR WOMEN

Question: When going to a job interview, is it acceptable for women to wear a slacks suit rather than a skirted suit?

Answer: It really depends on the type of company where you will be interviewing and the company location. If the company is known to be conservative, wear a skirted suit. If you know it has a business casual dress code on the day you will be there, a slacks suit should be fine.

WHEN YOU LAND THAT POSITION

Question: I interviewed a recent college graduate for a position at our architectural firm. She wore what I considered to be appropriate attire during both interviews. However, since she started working at our firm, her skirts have been much shorter than what she wore to the interview. What can I say to her to help her see that our company's expectations are for her to dress in the same professional manner that she did when she was interviewing with us?

Answer: If you are the personnel manager at your firm, I'd schedule time to meet with this person and share your company's dress code guidelines that state skirt length. If you don't have a documented dress code, put one in place immediately and distribute it to all employees, including this person.

WHEN YOU'RE NEW ON THE JOB

Q Question: I just landed a position, and I am attempting to buy a few outfits on a shoestring budget. I've only been to the office twice and saw very few people while I was there and I don't know what to buy. The person who hired me is on vacation for the next few weeks so I won't have a chance to speak with him about the company's dress code. What should I do?

A Answer: Try calling the human resources manager and have the dress code sent to you. If the company does not have a human resources department, the training department or secretary to the president may be able to get this information to you quickly. I would think that your interest in learning what is considered acceptable work attire would be most impressive to your organization. It would tell them that you want to adapt to their dress culture from the very start.

HOW TO LOOK PROMOTABLE

Q Question: I repeatedly hear my colleagues say things like "You have to look the part" and "It's important to look promotable." How do you look promotable? Isn't *performing* promotable what really matters? Please advise.

A **Answer:** I would agree with you when you say "acting promotable" is what really matters. If you want to climb the corporate ladder, your personal character and work performance are going to be the key factors in accomplishing that goal.

However, this doesn't mean that the way in which you present yourself is insignificant. While discussing the interview and hiring process, I once heard someone say, "No one has ever been hired solely based on what they wore to an interview; however, many have been rejected." I would dare to argue that being promoted falls into a similar category.

Very few, if any, individuals are promoted solely because of their professional image. But many individuals are overlooked when promotion time comes because they don't look the part. If you want to look promotable, I would challenge you to mirror your upper-level executives. Dress one level up—dress for the position you would like to have within your company.

CHAPTER 8

COMMANDING PRESENCE ON BUSINESS CASUAL DAYS

 THE 5 MOST COMMONLY MADE MISTAKES WHEN TRYING TO BUILD PRESENCE

1. Not commanding presence through your accessories or the way your clothes are maintained when dressing business casual.
2. Wearing business casual if there is a chance the individuals you will be meeting will be dressed in professional attire.
3. Not following the "one-notch-down" rule when dressing in business casual clothing.
4. Defining jeans as business casual rather than casual attire.
5. Wearing a shirt with a logo that does not pertain the organization you represent.

How can I command presence?

Question: What are some tips for commanding presence when dressing business casual?

Answer: My best advice for commanding presence when dressing business casual is to wear the best quality fabric you can afford. When it comes to accessories, buy high-quality merchandise. That includes investing in leather shoes, 14-karat gold, high-quality costume jewelry, silk scarves, and so forth. By investing in the best, you will command presence through your good taste.

When *not* to dress business casual

Question: When should business casual attire *not* be worn?

Answer: Business casual should not be worn when:

1. You are meeting individuals for the first time and are unsure of how they will be dressed.
2. You are interacting with individuals from outside the country.
3. You are involved in a performance appraisal.
4. You are delivering bad news.

5. You are up for a promotion and are meeting with the higher-ups to pitch yourself.
6. You are attending a function that is in a formal environment (wedding, funeral, graduation, etc.).

THE "ONE-NOTCH-DOWN" RULE

Q Question: Our company has gone business casual. While I really like being able to dress in a relaxed manner, I've noticed that some people show up for work looking sloppy. I'm afraid that if this continues, the business casual privilege will be taken away. What tips do you have to offer?

A **Answer:** Business casual is just what you said—a privilege. When this perk is not abused, it works well. Unfortunately, many employees equate business casual attire with not wearing well-maintained clothes. When they do this, they unknowingly sabotage their careers.

The way to make business casual work for you on business casual days is to follow the "one-notch-down" rule. In other words, wear one thing you wouldn't wear on business professional days. For instance, if a skirted suit is considered business professional in your organization, on business casual days, substitute the skirt for tailored slacks. While you may wear a different style shoe on business casual days than you would when dressed professionally, the quality of the shoe should remain the same.

By following this "one-notch-down" rule, you can be sure that your appearance will display your sense of professionalism.

WHY THE "ONE-NOTCH-DOWN" RULE WORKS

Q Question: I must thank you for sharing your "one-notch-down" rule in a workshop I attended. It is fool proof. I started a new job a few months after learning this rule and have been consistently following it. Shortly after I started in this new position, I was asked to fill in for my manager on two separate occasions. My manager shared that the reason I was asked to step in for him is because I am consistently professional in both my dress and actions.

A **Answer:** Congratulations for putting the "one-notch-down" rule into practice! It takes very little to show that you take your position seriously. It sounds like this rule has assisted you in making a positive impression by letting your manager know that you take pride in how you look on both business professional and business casual days.

"BLUE JEANS? THEY SHOULD BE WORN BY FARM GIRLS MILKING COWS."

—YVES ST. LAURENT

JEANS

Question: When a company's dress code says, "No blue jeans," would jeans that are not blue count?

Answer: Jeans are jeans. Consider the term "blue jeans" to refer to any sort of slacks made of denim.

SHIRTS WITH LOGOS

Question: Would you please address the issue of people showing up for work wearing shirts with logos? They look like they are sponsors of the product or service on the shirts.

Answer: Like you, many company's discourage wearing shirts with logos to work. It goes without saying that the only exception is wearing a shirt with the logo of the company you represent.

THE QUESTIONS

MOST COMMONLY ASKED BY MANAGERS

Question: How do you define business casual?

Answer: Although business casual cannot be universally defined, it does include having a clean, crisp, polished appearance. Even when dressing down, the clothes worn should never jeopardize one's professionalism.

Just as when you are dressed in business professional attire, your business casual clothes should assist you in projecting confidence and credibility. Unfortunately, business casual is often equated with throwing something together at the last minute.

Question: What role do managers play in maintaining a high standard of dress?

Answer: It goes without saying that managers should lead by example. If a manager waivers even slightly in his or her business casual dress, you can be sure that more employees will also go outside the parameters of what is expected of them when dressing down. Managers must always remember to model what they expect from others—and that includes the way they dress.

Question: What is the general perception of clients and customers when they see their vendors in business casual attire?

Answer: It really depends on whom you're asking and how your customers dress for work. In some instances, business casual attire lowers visual credibility. In other instances, clients who also wear business casual are pleased that vendors are "dressed down" because they do not feel underdressed.

Question: What have other companies experienced when adopting business casual policies?

Answer: Companies who clearly define their business casual expectations through documented guidelines and reminders to employees who dress inappropriately are pleased to have a more relaxed work environment. The organizations that find business casual to be a challenge are those who close their eyes to employees showing up for work inappropriately dressed.

Question: Some companies advertise business casual as a perk. Do employees see it this way?

Answer: Some employees see business casual as a perk. They believe it will cost them less to dress business casual (even if it is not necessarily the case). This is especially true if employees with direct client contact are also required to wear business professional on certain days.

Question: Please discuss the relationship between dress (such as image) and attitude (such as projecting and receiving).

Answer: Your overall appearance is a reflection of your end product or service. While managers may continue to maintain a professional "I-mean-business" attitude, individuals who are less seasoned may not know how to maintain that professional demeanor. In essence, their attitude may be more relaxed.

CHAPTER 9

WHAT TO WEAR DURING VIDEOCONFERENCES

 THE 5 MOST COMMONLY MADE VIDEOCONFERENCE DRESS MISTAKES:

1. Not recognizing that it is important to plan what you are going to wear for a videoconferences.
2. Not choosing a shirt and/or jacket that contrasts with the color of the walls.
3. Wearing jewelry that clinks and clanks.
4. Wearing shiny jewelry that may cause a reflection during the videoconference.
5. Dressing in casual attire when individuals from abroad will be participating in the videoconference.

The "Waist-up" Rule

Question: What exactly is the "waist-up" rule?

Answer: This rule means what it says: When deciding what to wear for a videoconference, the part of you that will be seen will be from the waist up, and that is the part you should dress accordingly. If you are spearheading the videoconference and will be giving a presentation by standing up, you will need to apply the "waist-up" rule to your entire body.

Key Rules

Question: What dress advice do you have for individuals participating in videoconferences?

Answer: Here are six key rules to follow when you know you will be part of a videoconference:

1. Check out the room where the videoconference is going to be held and the wall that will act as the backdrop. This will help you wear colors from the waist up that will contrast with the wall rather than having you blend in with it.
2. Play it safe by not wearing shirts or blouses with stripes, plaids, or prints. They tend to bleed on camera.

3. Keep jewelry and any other accessories that clink or clank at home that day. Even the slightest noise will be heard on camera.

4. Wear clothes that project authority—especially if the videoconference will reach clients and other individuals outside your company. What you say is very powerful; however, the way you look will add credibility to your words.

5. While most individuals wear glasses for enhancing their vision, if you have access to contacts lenses, consider wearing them during the videoconference to avoid any glare that may be caused from glasses.

6. Avoid wearing any large accessories that may cause an on-camera reflection. Examples include gold or silver necklaces, bracelets, and so forth.

COLORS TO AVOID

Q **Question: What colors should you make a point of not wearing during a videoconference?**

A **Answer:** The main colors to avoid during a videoconference are large portions of red, white, or black. The color red bleeds on camera, while white can give many people a washed-out look. Black doesn't test well on camera and should be avoided as well. Avoid wearing white because it tends to "burn out" on the camera. Various shades of blue test well on camera.

JEWELRY TO AVOID

Question: Should I make a point of not wearing certain jewelry?

Answer: Whatever you do, avoid wearing jewelry that can make noise during videoconferences. Besides causing noise pollution, if the jewelry is shiny, it may create a reflection during a videoconference.

"WILL THE PEOPLE IN THE CHEAPER SEATS CLAP YOUR HANDS? ALL THE REST OF YOU, JUST RATTLE YOUR JEWELRY."

–JOHN LENNON AT THE ROYAL FAMILY PERFORMANCE (NOVEMBER 4, 1963)

ADDING PRESENCE TO WHAT YOU WEAR DURING A VIDEOCONFERENCE

Question: What advice do you have for commanding presence through my attire during videoconferences?

Answer: My best advice is to wear a well pressed tailored outfit as well as a jacket. Make sure your clothes are well pressed and in a color compatible with the walls or backdrop where the videoconference is going to take place.

CHAPTER 10

HOW TO COMMAND THAT "21ST CENTURY" PRESENCE

 THE 5 MOST COMMONLY MADE "TURN-OF-THE-CENTURY" DRESS MISTAKES:

1. Wearing jeans with a shirt, tie or sport coat.
2. Not wearing clothes that give you "presence."
3. Dressing for the job you *have* rather than for the one you *want*.
4. Not letting your clothes help to identify your job status.
5. Wearing designer clothes as a form of oneupsmanship.

Dressing with Presence

Q Question: I'm in what I consider to be a rather peculiar situation. Six of the people in my department are much older than me. In fact, they are old enough to be my parents. Because many of them have particular areas of expertise, I frequently invite one or more of them to go with me to client meetings. Many of the clients usually confuse these individuals for the managers. When clients or suppliers learn that I am the department manager after directing much of the prior conversation to my employees, they find themselves rather embarrassed. What recommendations do you have so that I look like the boss?

A **Answer:** It sounds like you need "presence." I strongly recommend that you follow the "one-notch-up" rule when dressing for work. Wear one thing that will give your overall presence just a tad more clout than what the individuals in your department wear.

For example, when you are dressed professionally, wear a charcoal grey suit rather than a navy one. Subconsciously, a grey or black suit commands more authority than blue or taupe. When dressed business casual, wear a pair of tailored gabardine trousers (or skirt if you are a woman) with a crisp collared shirt, rather than wearing khakis.

Another foolproof way to dress like the top dog is to wear a sport coat or blazer. This piece of clothing is a surefire way for commanding the presence you seek.

By incorporating the "one-notch-up" rule into your professional style, you will help individuals whom with you are meeting for the first time to see that you are made of management material.

PACKAGING YOURSELF LIKE AN EXECUTIVE WHEN YOU'RE ON THE CLIMB

Q Question: What clothes do you suggest I wear to look like I'm on the fast track? I work for a tech company that is growing by leaps and bounds. I want to be one of the people who climb quickly within the organization. What clothes will project that image?

A Answer: Take a look at the last few people who have been promoted. Notice what your manager is wearing. What do these people wear? If these people's clothes are a notch above what you wear (such as a blazer that appears to be part of their daily attire), begin doing the same. By looking the part and being an excellent employee, you will be packaging yourself for climbing your organization's ladder of success.

HOW TO DRESS WITHOUT INTIMIDATING YOUR COLLEAGUES (AND EVEN YOUR BOSS)

Q Question: I have been blessed to come from a fairly well-heeled family. Now that I have graduated from college and am now beginning my career, I see that not everyone has the extensive designer wardrobe that my parents allowed me to buy for graduation. As much as I love Armani and Versace, I don't want to be the outsider based on what I wear. I love my job, so please don't suggest that I change my positions.

A **Answer:** Stick to the simple yet elegant clothes in your wardrobe, keeping the more flashy ones in your closet for weekend and evening wear. Unless you flaunt the designer names you've bought, your colleagues and boss may not even realize that your clothes are any different than theirs.

CHAPTER 11

TRAVEL AND DRESS: KEY WAYS FOR DRESSING ON THE RUN

 THE 5 MOST COMMONLY MADE MISTAKES IN DRESS WHILE TRAVELLING

1. Not owning luggage that makes travel easy.
2. Using luggage that looks less professional than the way you dress.
3. Not wearing an outfit that could get you through the next business day if the luggage you have checked gets lost.
4. Not carrying paperwork with you for out-of-town meetings.
5. Not packing clothes that mix and match with one another.

HAVE LUGGAGE, WILL TRAVEL

Q Question: My position will have me traveling out of town. Most of these trips will simply be for one to three nights at the most. What kind of luggage should I buy?

A **Answer:** Since your trips will be rather short in duration, I suggest that you invest in a soft-sided pullman on wheels. Invest in one that is large enough to hold a few outfits, yet small enough to meet airline requirements as carry-on baggage (approximately 45 inches overall). While you are investing in this piece, also consider buying a pullman that is the next size larger for longer trips.

BUT I LIKE THE LUGGAGE I HAVE

Q Question: My wife has been getting on my case about my luggage. She says that I should be ashamed of using it because it is so tattered. The reason it's so worn is due to the beating it takes from how it's handled by airport personnel after it's checked. I see no reason to buy new luggage when it will end up looking the same way over a short time. Help!

 Answer: I see both sides of this issue. Your wife is right in seeing that tattered luggage is a reflection of your overall look. At minimum, your luggage should be presentable. If it's as worn as you describe, it's time to either repair or replace it.

If your suitcase is damaged en route, most airlines will take care of the damage. When you decide to buy new luggage, be sure to inspect it carefully every time you remove it from the airport conveyer belt in baggage claim. If you see that your luggage has been damaged, file a report. Most airlines are more than willing to handle these claims.

ROAD WARRIOR ADVICE

Q Question: My job requires me to travel extensively. Often times, I'm gone for two weeks at a time. What advice do you have for road warriors?

A **Answer:** My best advice to you is to put together a travel wardrobe consisting of the same color. For instance, if you look good in black, invest in a black tailored jacket, long skirt, knee-length skirt, and slacks. Build your travel wardrobe around those pieces. You might add a red blazer, white blouse, sweater, multicolored scarves, or belts. Finally, take along gold-tone or silver-tone jewelry that is compatible with everything.

ALWAYS BE PREPARED

 Question: Throughout the years, my jobs have required me to travel extensively by air. However, early on I learned a lesson that I'd like to pass onto other less-seasoned business travelers. Always travel using the following rule: Either wear what would be appropriate to wear the following day or take a carry-on piece of luggage with you. Also, send any paperwork that you'll need for the meeting before you leave. Or carry a master copy of your material with you on the plane.

The reason I have found this rule to be such an important one is that before I began following it, I traveled to a city in casual clothes for an early-morning client meeting the following day. To my dismay, my luggage was not found and delivered to my hotel until hours after the meeting. Not only did I not have appropriate clothes to wear to the meeting, I was forced to show up there without the presentation material that was also in my suitcase.

Answer: Thank you for sharing these important words of wisdom for road warriors. You have emphasized the importance of always being prepared!

DRESS AS THOUGH YOU WERE GOING DIRECTLY TO THE MEETING

Question: What on-the-road dress tips do you have for traveling? When a colleague and I travel together, he always looks overdressed. I try to wear clothes that are comfortable. Which one of us is right?

Answer: Whatever you choose to wear en route, be sure to have on what you could wear if you were going directly to your meeting. Believe it or not, a lot of business contacts can be made when you're traveling. And when you look the part, people will be attracted to you. After all, if you're traveling on company time, you should wear what you would typically have on if you were going to a client meeting in your office.

IT'S ALL IN HOW YOU PACK

Question: How can I make my clothes work for me, instead of constantly working for my clothes?

Answer: First of all, make sure that the clothes you take on your trips pass the "scrunch" test. In other words, if you squeeze the garment and it wrinkles when you let go of it, leave it behind. Also, if time permits, unpack your clothes as soon as you check into your hotel room.

By doing so, you will give the clothes a chance to hang a bit. Finally, if there are still wrinkles in your clothes, try hanging them in the bathroom with the shower on and the door closed. You can be sure that any recent wrinkles will disappear. However, just about all hotel rooms have an iron and ironing board in a closet. When all else fails, iron away!

CHAPTER 12

THE ART OF DRESSING APPROPRIATELY WHEN DOING BUSINESS ABROAD

 THE 10 MOST COMMONLY MADE INTERNATIONAL DRESS MISTAKES:

1. Wearing shoes with rubber soles rather than those made of leather.
2. Dressing in flashy colors rather than in continental classic clothes.
3. Wearing several pieces of costume jewelry rather than a few of the real thing.
4. Wearing sleeveless tops in warm climates rather than shirts with sleeves.
5. Not recognizing that some colors are considered offensive in certain countries.
6. Wearing shorts and jeans in public.
7. Not recognizing that many international clients will equate your quality of clothes with the quality of work you can provide to them.
8. Wearing a striped tie when doing business in England and other countries of British influence.
9. Not recognizing that suits are more the norm than the exception abroad.

WHAT ABOUT SHOES?

Question: What are the rules for wearing certain types of shoes when traveling abroad?

Answer: In most countries other than the United States, shoes are made with leather soles rather than rubber ones. For men traveling abroad, shoes that tie rather than those that slip on (such as loafers) should be worn in business settings. Slip-on shoes (once again with leather soles) are typically worn in more casual settings. When traveling to countries where you will be visiting temples and mosques, it will be especially useful to wear slip-on shoes making it easy to take them on and off.

FOUR TIPS ON DRESSING FOR THE MAN ON THE INTERNATIONAL SCENE

Question: What dress advice do you have for men doing business abroad?

Answer: When traveling abroad, be sure to dress in a more conservative manner than you would in the United States. By following these four dress tips, you will represent both yourself and your organization in the best light:

1. Black is the color. Black suits, black shoes, black any-thing—black is the most appropriate color abroad.
2. Men should wear wing tips or other shoes with leather soles that tie rather than slip-ons.
3. Wear long-sleeved shirts. While a white shirt should be worn in conservative settings, you may want to have some colored shirts for less-formal business meetings.
4. Many countries are very designer conscious (such as France, Italy, Hong Kong, etc.) For that reason, be aware that quality jewelry, accessories, and even your pen will be noticed.

RULES FOR THE WORLDLY WOMAN

Question: My position requires me to travel internationally. What should I be sure to pack and which items should I leave behind?

Answer: Here are five dress rules for women travel-ling outside the United States:

1. Leave sleeveless tops at home. In many countries, it is considered a major faux pas to have your full arm showing.
2. Wear jewelry that is simple yet elegant. Quality is key.
3. Wear shoes that have a closed toe and avoid sling backs.
4. Always take both skirted suits and dresses with you rather than the slacks suits you may wear in the United States.

5. Either wear no nail polish or clear polish. Colored nail polish and fiberglass nails are much more the exception than the rule outside the United States.

GLOBETROTTER SHOES FOR WOMEN

Question: What about shoe styles for women when travelling internationally?

Answer: The best advice I can give you is to wear closed-toe shoes in high-quality hide with leather soles. You will be safest wearing pumps rather than sling-back shoes.

WHAT TO WEAR

Question: What kind of clothes should I take when traveling abroad? I'll be traveling to two continents over a period of a month and realize that I'll have to pack for different climates.

Answer: Take clothes that will allow you to dress in layers. Be sure these clothes are conservative in nature because most businesspeople outside the United States wear suits rather than business casual attire that is so prevalent here today. Be sure the clothes you take are dark colored rather than light or flashy.

LESS JEWELRY IS BETTER

 Question: I love jewelry. Any tips about what to take when traveling abroad?

Answer: There's a rule about taking jewelry on trips: "Whatever you take, be sure to wear." This will keep the items from being stolen. Also, you will be perceived in many countries as a better dresser by wearing fewer pieces that are higher in quality..

You will find that in many countries, 14-karat gold or silver jewelry is more prevalent than costume jewelry. That includes plastic jewelry for women and watches that beep for men.

> *"LET US NOT BE TOO PARTICULAR. IT IS BETTER TO HAVE OLD SECOND-HAND DIAMONDS THAN NONE AT ALL."*
>
> —MARK TWAIN, *FOLLOWING THE EQUATOR*

MINDING YOUR CLOTHING MANNERS

Question: What clothes are considered taboo items when travelling abroad?

Answer: Here's a short list that will keep you out of trouble:

1. Sleeveless tops.
2. Shorts, including Bermudas.
3. Jeans.
4. Hats worn in buildings (especially in temples, mosques, or churches).

COLORS TO AVOID?

Question: I've heard that many countries are rather superstitious about certain colors. Are there clothes in particular colors that I should leave at home?

Answer: You will do well traveling with darker clothes rather than flashy ones. Be sure to avoid wearing purple in Thailand as this is considered to be the color reserved for the monarchy. Neither should black be worn in Thailand because it implies that your mother has died. White is a color or mourning in China.

Forget the shorts and jeans

Question: When doing business abroad, what can I do to dispel the "Ugly American" reputation that North Americans tend to have?

Answer: If you're referring to dress, avoid wearing shorts and jeans in public. Also, when you are not working and want to dress casually, don't dress any less casually than a tailored shirt and khakis. If you are in a warmer climate, a polo shirt may be suitable.

Continental classic

Question: Are there certain clothing styles that you would consider to be accepted universally?

Answer: According to Robert and Melody Gensler, owners of Milwaukee's Sonny Boutique (for men) and Melody's Boutique (for women), "continental classic" is traditional classic clothing with a European flair. Often times, continental classic clothing is from Italy and Germany. Fabrics range from super wool, which is the best in gabardine, to luxury fabrics such as cashmere.

Quality is Key

Q Question: I've heard that designer clothes are noticed by international clients. Is that something that I should be conscious of when doing business abroad?

A Answer: You bet! Most countries are very conscious of clothes. For that reason, the quality of clothes you wear will be noticed. By dressing in a professional yet understated manner, you will represent yourself well and also be a reflection of the quality of work you provide.

Avoiding striped ties in Anglicized Countries and other tie issues

Q Question: What recommendations do you have when wearing ties abroad?

A Answer: As with the other clothes you wear, quality is key. Wear ties that are made of 100 percent silk. When you are doing business in England or other countries of British influence, avoid wearing striped ties. They just may be similar to one's regiment.

WHAT CLOTHES TO TAKE

Question: What kind of clothes should I pack for going abroad?

Answer: In most countries, men will be safe wearing suits with white shirts. In more conservative countries, white shirts with ties are more appropriate. However, in less conservative settings, darker-colored shirts with ties may be worn.

In very hot climates (such as Thailand), you may want to wear short-sleeved colored shirts with ties once your meet with your Thai contacts and notice that they are dressed accordingly.

CHAPTER 13

OUT AND ABOUT

 THE 6 MOST COMMON MISTAKES MADE WHEN STEPPING OUT

1. Overdressing for a holiday function.
2. Underdressing for a holiday gathering.
3. Wearing a skirt or dress that may be too short.
4. Showing up in a blouse that is too low-cut.
5. Wearing clothes that are seductive.
6. Not recognizing what "dressy-formal" means.

WHEN YOU LIVE IN THE SAME NEIGHBORHOOD WHERE YOU WORK

Q Question: I work for a very conservative law firm and dress the part each day meeting its expectations. I especially like working there because it's within walking distance from where I live. However, what I don't like is that I'm always running into someone from the firm on evenings and weekends and feel as though I am losing my privacy.

When I do run into senior partners, they look at my clothes as though I'm not dressed appropriately for work. However, what seems to freak them out the most are my tattoos and my nose ring (that I make a point of not wearing during the workday). What can I do to not jeopardize my job without losing my sense of self during my personal time?

A **Answer:** You have two choices: Either find a place to live that is not in the same neighborhood where you work or change your dress habits by eliminating the nose ring and making your tattoos not visible. If you continue to display two contrasting images you are bound to jeopardize your future within this organization.

HOLIDAY OFFICE PARTY OUTFIT NO-NOS

 Question: When invited to a holiday gathering, what should I wear?

Answer: First of all, what does the invitation state? If recommended attire is not listed, ask a colleague who has good taste and who attended the function the year before. When all else fails, remember that you can never get in trouble looking conservative. For instance, if the gathering is at the office, try wearing a skirt or a slacks suit. The same applies when you are invited to co-worker's home. The main rule to follow is this: Don't go too short or too low. Whatever you do, *never* wear peek-a-boo see-through tops!

"ELEGANCE IS GOOD TASTE PLUS A DASH OF DARING."

—CARMEL SNOW, FORMER EDITOR OF *HARPER'S BAZAAR* IN HER BIOGRAPHY, *THE WORLD OF CARMEL SNOW*

"SHE WORE JUST ENOUGH FOR MODESTY—NO MORE."

—ROBERT BUCHANAN, *WHITE ROSE AND RED*

WHAT TO WEAR TO A HOLIDAY PARTY

Q Question: I am going to a company holiday party this weekend and I am not sure what is appropriate to wear. It is semi-formal and our regular dress is business casual Monday through Thursday and casual on Friday. How sexy a dress is appropriate for the party?

A **Answer:** When going to a semi-formal function, wear something elegant and festive. For instance, a black crepe, silk, or even a velvet skirt, dress, or slacks suit would be elegant. Whatever you do, please do not sabotage your career by wearing anything that may be interpreted as sexy.

"NOTHING GOES OUT OF FASHION SOONER THAN A LONG DRESS WITH A VERY LOW NECK."

—COCO CHANEL (1883-1971) IN MARCEL HAEDRICH'S BIOGRAPHY, *COCO CHANEL: HER LIFE, HER SECRETS*

FABRICS WORN AT BLACK-TIE FUNCTIONS

Question: When going to black-tie holiday functions, are there certain fabrics to wear?

Answer: Go for the simple yet elegant fabrics. When attending formal affairs, look for outfits in silk, crepe, or satin (for those winter galas). While a velvet outfit limits your wear, since this fabric should only be worn between November and March, clothes made in this material look regal.

THE HOSTESS WITH THE MOSTEST

Question: What is proper attire when entertaining business associates in my home?

Answer: Because you are hosting the gathering, what you encourage others to wear through your invitation will set the tone for what's appropriate. Be sure to follow suit.

WHEN ATTENDING

GATHERINGS IN A HOME

Question: How am I supposed to know what to wear to a holiday gathering in someone's home?

Answer: When in doubt, call and ask the person hosting the function. If you are not able to reach the person, ask someone who has been to these types of functions. You will be safe if you err on the side of conservative dress.

DRESSY-FORMAL

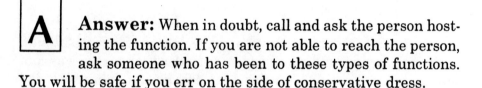

Question: What exactly does the term "dressy-formal" mean?

Answer: I would define the term "dressy-formal" to mean the same as semi-formal. In other words, wear clothes that are a notch above business professional.

For men, that may mean to wear a black suit, white shirt, and silk tie. For women, it would be defined as wearing a dress or slacks suit in a crepe, silk, or other dressy fabric.

In some instances, "dressy-formal" may even be defined as men wearing a tuxedo and women wearing a long gown. It's always better to play it safe by asking what is listed on the invitation sent to you or calling the person hosting the function if "dressy-formal" is not defined clearly.

CHAPTER 14

DRESS CODE GUIDELINE FINDINGS

In 1999, a survey was conducted by At Ease Inc. with human resource directors and training directors. Another survey was conducted by At Ease Inc. in Spring 1999. Respondents included human resource directors and training managers from banks, airlines, online companies, travel agents, educational institutions, high-tech firms, health care institutions, credit unions, and more. Here are the findings:

1. *75 PERCENT OF HUMAN RESOURCE MANAGERS AND TRAINING MANAGERS SAID THAT THEIR ORGANIZATIONS DO HAVE A WRITTEN DRESS CODE.*

2. *WHEN ASKED, "HOW DOES YOUR ORGANIZATION DEFINE BUSINESS CASUAL FOR MEN," RESPONSES INCLUDED:*

- ◆ No jeans. Polo shirt and Docker-style pants (this would be the lowest standard).
- ◆ No ties. Slacks and polo shirt.
- ◆ No jeans. No offensive logo t-shirts.
- ◆ Not defined.
- ◆ Blue jeans and sport shoes are not permitted in offices, though both are allowed in our labs and plants. Shorts are not permitted anywhere.
- ◆ Dress slacks; no t-shirts.

Jeans or other casual slacks (except cargo), casual shoes, polo shirts, sweaters, no ties.

Businesslike slacks, polo-type sport shirts and sweaters.

No jeans. Shirt with collar. No denim and no sandals.

Collared shirt. No denim, fleece,sneakers or sandals.

Long pants, sport coat, dress shirt, slacks, polo shirt, sweater.

The following are prohibited: Spandex, torn or dirty jeans, shorts or painted slacks, jogging suits, sweatshirts, tank tops, clothing with slogans.

Sport coat, slacks, polo shirt, sweaters.

Navy blazer with tan khaki slacks.

Slacks, sport shirts (cotton/knit), sweater and turtleneck. Neat jeans may also be worn.

Casual slacks, sweater, shirts with collars.

Does not define business casual, this exists only on Friday for management.

Golf shirts / shirts with collars or any company logo shirt. No jeans, no sneakers, socks are required.

3. WHEN ASKED, "HOW DOES YOUR ORGANIZATION DEFINE BUSINESS CASUAL FOR WOMEN?" RESPONSES INCLUDED:

No jeans. Polo shirt and Docker-style pants (this would be the lowest standard).

No shorts, no jeans.

Not defined.

Blue jeans and sport shoes are not permitted in offices, though both are in our labs and plants. Shorts are not permitted anywhere.

No nylons, jeans, other casual slacks (except cargo), casual shirts, or sweaters.

Dresses or suits, businesslike skirts, blouses, sweaters, or shorts sets. No tennis shoes, no sneakers.

No jeans, no denim. Hosiery/slacks. No sandals.

Variable, dress identified in policy (appropriate and inappropriate).

◆ No shorts, denim, fleece, or sneakers.
◆ Slacks, sweater, skirts. Jeans only acceptable on Friday if you pay $1 to the United Way.
◆ Casual pants suits, jackets, sweaters, slacks, polo shirts.
◆ Blazer with slacks or shirt.
◆ Slacks, skirts, dresses and blouses, sweater, and turtleneck. Neat jeans may also be worn.
◆ Casual slacks, skirts, or shorts, appropriate tops, sweaters, or shirts. Jeans, only on Fridays. Prohibited: Jeans not in good condition, T-shirt, sweats, tank tops, bare back, off-the-shoulder tops, sandals without socks or hose.
◆ Blouses or collared shirts.

4. WHEN ASKED, "IF YOUR ORGANIZATION DOES NOT HAVE A WRITTEN DRESS CODE, HOW DO EMPLOYEES KNOW WHAT IS CONSIDERED 'APPROPRIATE' DRESS?" ANSWERS INCLUDED:

We model after our boss.
They are given that information on their first day.
Business casual, never jeans or t-shirt.
It is discussed at the time of hire.
Subject to supervisor/manager judgment.
By observing what others wear or by asking supervisor.
They sometimes don't!
Dictated by management.
Dress guidelines are given to each employee.
Policies are written and shared with associates in the orientation.
Observation; guidance from peers and management.
By examples set by management.

5. WHEN ASKED, "IF AN EMPLOYEE IS DRESSED INAPPROPRIATELY FOR WORK, HOW IS THE SITUATION HANDLED?" ANSWERS INCLUDED:

21 percent of respondents said, "Nothing is said to the person."
21 percent of respondents said, "It becomes part of office gossip."

84 percent of respondents said, "The manager addresses the issue with the person."

6. WHEN ASKED HOW THE TOPIC OF INAPPROPRIATE DRESS IS COMMUNICATED:

63 percent of respondents said "Behind closed doors."
3 percent of respondents said "In a voice-mail message."
12 percent of respondents said "Through an e-mail message."
22 percent of respondents answered:
Through a follow-up e-mail reminder of policy to the entire group.
Through the human resources representative.
We have very few closed doors, so it is handled discretely, although managers are not the best at enforcing it unless someone outside the group (such as HR) points out something inappropriate.
Employee could be sent home for a change of clothing.
Some managers address it immediately; some let it go.
The HR rep. may discuss with employee or employee's manager.
The person will be sent home to change and not paid for absent time.
Through pre-class meeting.
We also cover the issue in new associate training orientation and in training.
It usually shows up in our communication box as an "issue to be resolved."

7. WHEN ASKED, "IF YOU WERE GIVEN THE RESPONSIBILITY OF CHANGING YOUR BUSINESS CASUAL POLICY BACK TO BUSINESS PROFESSIONAL DRESS, HOW WOULD YOU MAKE THIS CHANGE?"

18 percent of respondents said, "I would begin by instituting Mondays as 'dress-up' days."
9 percent of respondents said, "I would make the change by offering a company-paid uniform that consisted of a

shirt, navy blazer, and trousers for men and a navy blazer and skirt or tailored slacks for women.

63 percent of respondents' answers are included the following comments:

◆ Through a written policy, tip sheets, video program for training.

◆ I wouldn't do it. The degree to which people are considered professional is not related to a particular set of garments but is an outgrowth of their character and integrity.

◆ Announcement effective 1/99. We haven't been business casual that long.

  Written policy giving specific "allowed/not allowed."

  Write the policy so it was clear and do some video training that has specific cxamples.

  I would have the message relayed by the president to ensure full involvement.

  I would resign before I had to do it!

  Issue new guidelines.

  Would begin with salesforce, as this would be customer-driven for my company.

  Explaining reasons; describe appropriate and inappropriate examples of dress.

  At my company, summer is "business casual," the rest of the year is "business professional."

  A combination of company-logo apparel and professional dress.

◆ Institute jeans on Friday.

◆ Change it all together in one action; probably would never do this because employees love business casual!

◆ We have very few casual days.

◆ I believe a large percentage of our employees would prefer uniforms.

◆ I would announce the change effective in 90 days.

◆ Inform everyone that due to (whatever reason) effect, the company dress code will be as follows (describe dress code).

8. WHEN ASKED HOW THEIR ORGANIZATION'S DRESS CODE WILL CHANGE DURING THE NEXT FIVE TO 10 YEARS...

54 percent of respondents said, "I predict our dress code will remain as it is."

18 percent of respondents said, "I foresee that business casual attire will only be allowed for individuals who do not have direct customer contact."

12 percent of respondents said, "I believe that business professional attire will no longer be worn by individuals in management."

3 percent of respondents said "I foresee that jeans will be worn by everyone in our company."

27 percent of respondents shared one of more of these comments:

"I foresee that jeans will be worn by everyone in our company at times."

"We are currently dressing business casual for both nonmanagement and management employees."

"It will be changed slightly."

"It may be industry specific (as it is now). We are in the automotive field, which is business casual all the way up the line."

"I foresee business casual dress being allowed on three or four days throughout the year."

"We review policy annually for needed changes or suggested modifications. Women's fashions are reviewed."

"As a manufacturing company in the Southwest, I don't see us becoming more formal again."

"Develop a cross-functional team to determine the purpose, process, payoff, communication, culture issues, and implementation plan."

9. WHEN ASKED, "HOW HAS YOUR ORGANIZATION'S DRESS CODE CHANGED DURING THE LAST 10 YEARS?" ANSWERS INCLUDED:

Casual day observed/casual day revoked 4/99.

We now have "Casual Fridays."

It has gotten very relaxed.

Business too casual—and just casual.

From business attire to corporate casual.

We now have a casual-attire day every Friday.

Business to business casual.

Dress-down day once a month. As a bank we keep to tight guidelines.

We have gone from traditional business attire to casual business attire.

Changed from suits/dresses to business casual.

The dress code has become more relaxed and casual.

More informal.

Informal business is now the norm.

Adapted a business casual dress policy

Casual Friday; no open-toed shoes.

Service employees can wear shorts. Became more relaxed, dress-down Fridays—casual dress, when classes are over—no ties are required.

Informal business attire is now the norm.

10. WHEN ASKED, "IF YOUR ORGANIZATION'S DRESS CODE HAS NOT CHANGED DURING THE LAST 10 YEARS, WHY HASN'T IT CHANGED?" RESPONDENTS ANSWERED:

I want my employees to look like professionals.

We had a new administration.

It started with casual Friday, evolved to all casual except for customer meetings.

By trying to offer benefits that other companies are offering, like casual Fridays.

Other banks in town did it.

Our employees requested it.

We went from Friday dress down (casual) to always casual (unless meeting with customers).

Because of a changing corporate culture.

From employee feedback and trends in the marketplace.

The changed occurred based on what similar
companies in our area have done.

Employee influences and influence of "peer"
companies in industry.

Employee dissatisfaction.

The CEO is very traditional and requires traditional
dress.

Changed to business casual for customers. Felt we
needed to be "on the same level" or more approachable.

Jeans on Friday is now extended to everyday.

Gradual for first five years.

Our new CEO implemented change.

As our company expanded, nicer clothes were
expected.

Employee input; safety/risk management.

The change was gradual for the first five years.

Finally, a deliberate decision was announced. Our
customers' dress code was a big influence.

**11. WHEN ASKED, "IF YOUR ORGANIZATION'S DRESS CODE HAS
CHANGED DURING THE LAST 10 YEARS, WHAT BENEFITS DO YOU BELIEVE
HAVE OCCURRED AS A RESULT OF THIS CHANGE?" RESPONDENTS' AN-
SWERS INCLUDED:**

More relaxed, feeling of choice—use your judgment,
more control.

A "free" additional benefit to our employees.

None. It lowered productivity.

It removed the "we/they" from our culture.

Employees are more comfortable and relaxed.

It tends to help perceptions of senior management as
being "real" people and fosters teamwork.

Other than comfort for employees, I don't see any
benefits.

More relaxed atmosphere, greater comforts, more
diversity of style and expression.

Employees work better when more comfortable.

Casual Day is viewed as a special treat. It adds fun to the day.

It increases comfort and allows employees to fit in better with customers. They appear more approachable.

Less costly for employees.

More relaxed atmosphere.

Employees are happier and more relaxed.

The relaxed atmosphere is enjoyed by all.

I prefer not to wear uniforms. However, uniforms are a cost savings on my personal budget.

Employees enjoy casual option for Friday; morale is increased.

Happier workforce, more comfortable on the job.

We fit in with the rest of the area.

More relaxed work environment—friendlier, less positioning.

12. WHEN ASKED, "IF YOUR ORGANIZATION'S DRESS CODE HAS NOT CHANGED DURING THE LAST 10 YEARS, WHAT BENEFITS DO YOU BELIEVE YOUR COMPANY HAS HAD AS A RESULT OF IT REMAINING THE SAME?" RESPONDENTS ANSWERED:

We present a professional front to the community.

◆ Our dress code is clearly communicated.

We have kept the image of a professional travel agency.

13. WHEN ASKED, "IF YOUR ORGANIZATION'S DRESS CODE HAS CHANGED DURING THE LAST 10 YEARS, WHAT DISADVANTAGE(S) HAVE YOU NOTED AS A RESULT OF THIS DRESS CODE CHANGE?" RESPONDENTS ANSWERED:

◆ Some employees resented what they thought was a loss of an employee benefit.

◆ Some go overboard and use poor judgment.

◆ A few employees have taken business casual Friday to the extreme.

It has lowered productivity on Fridays.

I believe it has created an atmosphere of extreme familiarity that has brought on unprofessional behavior. Also, with no official rules, it is hard to object to something I believe to exceed good taste.

Some people don't observe policies. When guests visit, we don't all look our best.

Employees try to bend the rules too much.

Somewhat of a more relaxed atmosphere.

Some take "casual" to the extreme—have to post notice when customers come in for important meetings.

I believe the staff acts more relaxed and casual (less professional) and do not distinguish between their roles at home and the office.

At times, too informal.

More relaxed atmosphere! Employees tend to dress too far "down."

Some employees are a bit too casual.

An unprofessional image.

Some people's tastes are questionable regarding "appropriate" casual wear.

Some people going to extreme "casual."

It allows for a more relaxed work environment—less formal, less considerate of personal/professional space.

14. WHEN ASKED, "IF YOUR ORGANIZATION'S DRESS CODE HAS CHANGED DURING THE LAST 10 YEARS, HOW DO YOUR EMPLOYEES FEEL ABOUT THIS CHANGE?" RESPONDENTS ANSWERED:

Almost everyone likes it.

They like the change.

Most personnel like it.

It's been positive for the most part.

They seem to enjoy the change.

Employees like being able to dress as they wish.

They like it! They defend it and protest when any hint of change occurs.

They like the flexibility to dress for whatever their day may be (golf, meetings, dinner meetings, etc.).

They are trying to adjust by buying coordinating accessories to help individualize their wardrobe.

Casual Day has been positive.

Closed-toe shoes have met some resistance.

◆ Great! They asked for the changes and love them.

They love it!

No one complains!

15. WHEN ASKED, "WHAT IS CONSIDERED BUSINESS PROFESSIONAL DRESS FOR MEN ACCORDING TO YOUR ORGANIZATION'S STANDARDS?" RESPONDENTS ANSWERED:

A shirt, tie, jacket (if work requires).

A suit, white or blue dress shirt, tie, leather tie shoes.

A coat and tie.

A suit and tie of conservative taste.

A suit, tie, dress shirt.

A shirt, tie, and suit preferred.

A suit or sportcoat, slacks, shirt, and tie.

Generally, Dockers and a nice shirt. For special meetings, a suit and tie.

Casual slacks and a shirt with collar.

Shirts with collar; dress pants (tie optional).

A suit, tie, and sport coat.

A golf shirt or an open collared shirt with jeans, casual pants, or Bermuda shorts

Khaki or navy slacks with a white knit short-sleeved golf shirt.

Dress shirt, trousers and tie.

Dress shirt and tie / sportcoat or suit coat optional.

ABOUT THE AUTHOR

Ann Marie Sabath is the president of At Ease Inc., a 15-year-old Cincinnati-based company specializing in domestic and international business etiquette programs. She is also the author of *Business Etiquette In Brief*; *Business Etiquette: 101 Ways to Conduct Business With Charm And Savvy*; *International Business Etiquette: Asia & The Pacific Rim*; and *International Business Etiquette: Europe*. Her fifth book, *International Business Etiquette: Latin America* was released in bookstores internationally in January 2000.

Sabath's international and domestic etiquette concepts have been featured in *The Wall Street Journal, USA Today*, and Delta Airlines' *Sky Magazine*. They also have been recognized on *The Oprah Winfrey Show* and *20/20*.

Since 1987, Sabath and her staff have trained more than 40,000 individuals representing the business, industry, government, and educational sectors in how to gain a competitive edge. Her "10 Key Ways for Enhancing Your Global Savvy," "Polish That Builds Profits," and "Business Etiquette: The Key to Effective Services" programs have been presented to individuals from Deloitte & Touche L.L.P., Fidelity Investments, General Electric, Procter & Gamble, Arthur Andersen, MCI Telecommunications, Marriott International, Salomon Brothers, MIT, Columbia University, and Miami University, among hundreds of others.

In 1992, At Ease Inc. became an international firm by licensing its concept in Taiwan. In 1998, it also established its presence in Egypt, Australia, and Slovakia by certifying individuals in these countries.

FOR MORE INFORMATION

You have read that it takes a lot more than simply "knowing the ropes" in order to successfully climb that slippery ladder of success in business. Getting dressed in the morning is both an art and a science. I hope that you will refer to this book often to sharpen your skills.

Do you have a question about business dress that was not addressed in this book? You can e-mail me at:

beyondbusinesscasual@atease.com

Or, you can write to me at:

At Ease Inc.
119 East Court Street
Cincinnati, OH
45202

You may also have your questions answered by calling my hotline at (800)873-9909. You can be assured of a prompt response.

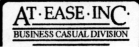

AT·EASE·INC·
BUSINESS CASUAL DIVISION

Beyond Business Casual HOTLINE

WHAT BUSINESS DRESS QUESTIONS DO YOU HAVE?
The Real Definition of Business Casual • Resort Casual
Accessories Etiquette • On The Road Attire • Image Tips
• Holiday Dress • International Dress

E-Mail Your Questions To: beyondbusinesscasual@ateaseinc.com
or Call Our U.S. Domestic Hotline At (800) 873-9909
For Calls From Outside The U.S., dial (513) 241-5216
Or Fax Your Questions To (513) 241-8701
Visit Our Website at http:www.corporateetiquette.com
119 East Court Street • Cincinnati, Ohio 45202

RESOURCES

At Ease Inc. *The "Where Have All The Dress Rules Gone?" Video Series*. Cincinnati: At Ease Inc., 1999.

Amiel, Irene. *Business Casual Made Easy*. Falls Church, VA: Business Casual Publications, 1999.

Bonnell, Kimberly. *What to Wear:A Style Handbook*. Chicago: Griffin Trade Paperback, 1999.

Greenleaf III, Clinton T. *Attention to Detail: A Gentleman's Guide to Professional Appearance and Conduct*. Chesterland, OH: Greenleaf Enterprises, 1998.

Svlavik, Christopher. *The Indispensable Guide to Classic Men's Clothing*. Blacksburg, VA: Tetra Press, 1999.

Maysonave, Sherry. *Casual Power: How To Power Up Your Nonverbal Communication & Dress Down for Success*. Akron, IN: Bright Books Inc., 1999.

Molloy, John T. *New Women's Dress for Success*. Boston: Warner Books Inc., 1996.

Nicolson, Joanna. *Dressing Smart in the New Millennium*. Greenwich, CT: Impact Publications, 1999.

Pooser, Doris. *Successful Style: A Man's Guide to a Complete Professional Image*. Menlow Park, CA: Crisp Publication, 1988.

Pooser, Doris. *Secrets of Style*. Menlow Park, CA: Crisp Publications, 1994.

Pooser, Doris. *Always In Style*. Menlow Park, CA: Crisp Publications, 1997.

Seitz, Victoria A. *Your Executive Image: The Art of Self-Packaging for Men and Women*. Holbrook, MA: Bob Adams Inc., 1992.

Snelianuk, Scott. *Esquire's Things a Man Should Know About Style*. Berkeley, CA: Riverhead Books, 1999.

Payne, Wilbert W. *The Classic Look Video*. Walnut Creek, CA: Star Image International, 2000.

Weber, Mark and The Van Heusen Creative Design Group. *Dress Casually for Success...For Men*. Highstown, NJ: McGraw-Hill, 1997.

INDEX

0-595-30653-5

TT 507 .S212 2004
Sabath, Ann Marie.
Beyond Business Casual: What to Wear to
work if

DATE DUE

GAYLORD			PRINTED IN U.S.A.

Printed in the United States
49302LVS00005B/97-99

9 780595 306534